"Pursue your dream and make your life a masterpiece."

— Ruben Gonzalez

Ruben Gonzalez
Salt Lake City Olympics, 84 MPH

BECOMING
UNSTOPPABLE
How to be an Olympian in Business and in Life

RUBEN GONZALEZ

CONTACT RUBEN
To book Ruben to speak at your next meeting, conference, or function, call:
832-689-8282

For more information, visit:
www.TheOlympicSpeaker.com

Becoming Unstoppable
By Ruben Gonzalez

Printed in the United States of America - MMVIII

Cover Design by Marily Jacob
Editing by Patti McKenna

ISBN 978-0-9781233-5-2

Published by: Aspen Publishing
Houston, TX
832-689-8282

What Other Top Achievers are Saying about Ruben Gonzalez' Work...

"Ruben Gonzalez achieved what few people ever do: mastery of his will. Motivating and inspiring!"

Dr. Stephen Covey - Author *"The 7 Habits of Highly Effective People"*

"Ruben speaks from both his head and his heart and inspires ordinary people, convincing them they can do extraordinary things. He is persuasive, enthusiastic, and <u>very</u> real. Invite him to present his ideas to your group, and you will glad you did."

Zig Ziglar - Author *"See You at the Top"*

"I was there for the Miracle on Ice in Lake Placid in 1980 and, again, for the miracle on the mountain in Utah in 2002. No Olympian I have ever met has more of what makes a champion than Ruben Gonzalez. Read and internalize, and you will realize and materialize your own dreams!"

Dr. Denis Waitley - Author *"The Psychology of Winning"*

"If you will read or listen to Ruben speak, your life will change for the positive."

Lou Holtz - Legendary Notre Dame Football Coach Author *"Winning Every Day"*

"This is truly a blueprint to success. Read it, apply its timeless lessons, and you'll transform your dreams into reality."

The Honorable Bob McEwen - U.S. Congressman

"Ruben teaches us that once we transform our fear into energy we begin to transform our dreams into reality."

Gerhard Gschwandtner - Founder and Publisher,
Selling Power Magazine

"Ruben's not only earned his spurs, but he's for real. His thankful spirit and his humble attitude makes him one of the most wonderful speakers, most genuine speakers I have heard in my life, and I recommend him with all my heart to you."

Charlie "Tremendous" Jones – Author *"Life is Tremendous"*

"Ruben Gonzalez' exciting story of hard work, dedication and commitment – leading to success and achievement in the greatest competition in the world – is inspiring and uplifting in a wonderful way!"

Brian Tracy - Author *"Million Dollar Habits"*

"Ruben is a testament to the power of the human spirit. His book is a passionate call to action, challenging you to be the best that you can be. Through his amazing Olympic story, Ruben will inspire you to pursue your dream, equip you to get through the struggle and encourage you on to victory."

Rudy Ruettiger – Inspiration for the movie *"Rudy"*

"Inspirational! Ruben has a unique ability to motivate and challenge his audiences. His compelling story about triumph over adversity on the road to the Olympics provokes us all to set and reach lofty goals."

Jack Canfield – Author *"The Success Principles"*

"Practical advice that will energize and empower you to succeed. Ruben hits you with the absolute truth about what it takes to succeed in the real world."

Jim Rohn - America's Foremost Business Philosopher

"Ruben's message of Determination, Commitment and Persistence struck home with our sales organization. His Inspirational message proves he is a winner, not only in the greatest sporting competition of all, but also in team motivation. He is living testament to the concept of "Never Quit!""

Jerry Farmer - VP North American Sales Xerox

"Olympian Ruben Gonzalez knows what it takes to be a winner. In clear, concise and straightforward language, his book, *Becoming Unstoppable*, steers you through all the important action steps so that you can become a winner, too!"

Paul J. Meyer - Founder of Success Motivation International and New York Times best-selling author

"Terrific! Ruben is a true Rhino! His crystal-clear vision of success cuts through all boundaries. Ruben challenges us to do more, be more, take more chances, and ultimately live life to the max."

Scott Alexander - Author *"Rhinoceros Success"*

"Ruben Gonzalez tells the readers that on the journey to success quitters never win and winners never quit. You will be inspired to action once you have read Ruben's *Becoming Unstoppable*. This book is a must read."

Don M. Green - Executive Director Napoleon Hill Foundation

"Ruben Gonzalez is a transformer! He mastered the principles of transforming his own life, becoming an Olympian, and now a successful speaker and author. The principles he mastered are here for your taking in an accessible and believable format. He does it and he teaches it."

Dave Ramsey - New York Times best-selling author *"The Total Money Makeover,"* National Radio Talk Show Host

"Ruben has lived what he teaches. He knows how to get to the top... and more importantly, how to stay there. His book *Becoming Unstoppable* lays out a flight plan with exactly what to do to reach your personal and professional goals. Read it, apply its timeless principles, and you'll achieve more than ever before."

Howard Putnam - Former CEO Southwest Airlines, Author *"The Winds of Turbulence"*

"Ruben Gonzalez' personal experiences with turning dreams into goals, then into reality...and his contagious fire of enthusiasm will inspire, encourage and direct you into improved performance. Invite him to speak for your organization and your people will experience a newness of life!"

Ed Foreman - U.S. Congressman (rtd.) Texas and New Mexico; Author, Speaker and Entrepreneur

"Ruben Gonzalez understands that what makes a person unstoppable is the pursuit of the dream. Herein lie the words that can lead you to greatness and to the very moment when you decide to be......unstoppable!"

James H. Amos Jr. - Chairman and CEO Tasti D-Lite, Chairman Emeritus Mail Boxes Etc./ The UPS Store

The #1 question people ask me after listening to my speeches is:

"How can I be more successful and get better results in everything I do?"

This book is the answer to that question.

This Book Could Change Your Life!
(but only if you apply it's information)

Following these five tips will help you turn this information into habits that will change your life:

1. **Read this book more than once.** I've read both "Think and Grow Rich" and "The Magic of Thinking Big" every year for the last 20 years. The more times you read a book, the more you become like the book.

2. **Underline and make notes.** Have a pen and highlighter in your hand. Underlining specific lines and paragraphs will triple your retention rate. Write your own thoughts in the margins and own this book.

3. **Re-read your underlines.** Re-read your key items over and over. Record and listen to your notes.

4. **Apply the material <u>immediately.</u>** Doing so will help you understand the material better. Don't try to be perfect. Done is better than perfect.

5. **Prioritize what you want to learn.** Select one to three things from the book, apply them faithfully and make them a habit.

This book is dedicated to my parents,
who taught me the values and principles
that helped me realize my dreams.

CONTENTS

Part V – Committing to Your Dream

Part VI – Overcoming Challenges on the Way to the Top

Part VII – Becoming all that You Can Be as You Cross the Finish Line

Foreword by
Congressman Bob McEwen

Three-time Olympian Ruben Gonzalez is an inspired speaker and author. Ruben has written a book hard to match: one that speaks to you. I believe that as you read Ruben's common sense ideas, you will think he's *right there, by your side*, sharing his insights, pointing you up the right path. *Becoming Unstoppable* is more than just a book; it's a blueprint to success.

Ruben's message in *Becoming Unstoppable* is representative of my own philosophy: "America is the land of opportunity; and, as Americans, it is our responsibility to use our God-given talents in the pursuit of our hopes and dreams."

Ruben will help you identify your dream. Then, he'll help you discover your strengths. Finally, he'll be by your side as you use those strengths to realize your dreams. *Becoming Unstoppable* does more than tell Ruben's personal views on success. Ruben will get you to see that reaching your dream is possible, and then he'll inspire you and equip you to take the necessary steps to realizing your dream. After reading this book and applying its ideas, you'll be committed to your dream and you'll be walking like…a champion!

Becoming Unstoppable comes to life, because Ruben has written this book straight from his life experiences. An accomplished athlete and entrepreneur, Ruben pressed his way through the unfounded judgments of skeptics, broken bones, and zero sponsorship to become an Olympian...three times over! In three different decades! Ruben is candid and transparent about his difficulties and his successes in this book, and is just as candid and just as transparent about how his tenacious bulldog spirit transformed him into a winner.

There's a champion in all of us. Whether you're a struggling salesperson, an entrepreneur building a business, a student looking for better grades or a coach seeking to motivate your entire team to the state title, *Becoming Unstoppable* will speak to you.

Be like Ruben. Be an overcomer. Become an achiever. Realize your full potential. Learn how to be a determined leader. Create that winning frontrunner mentality. Create your own your success story...right now. Become an Olympian on your own turf.

Read *Becoming Unstoppable*. Read it carefully. Take it seriously. Follow through like Ruben. Do what Ruben says. Do what Ruben does.

If you do what I say and carefully, seriously read this book, *Becoming Unstoppable*, **and** follow through with all of Ruben's good instruction, then you really **will** realize your goals and dreams!

The Honorable Bob McEwen - U.S. Congressman

A Word from the Author

My Dad always told me, "If you read about the lives of people you admire, you'll learn what works and what doesn't work in life, because success leaves clues."

That was some of the best advice I've ever had. Over the years I've read hundreds of biographies, always looking for clues that would help me achieve my dreams and ambitions. Along the way I learned that successful people think differently. They have conditioned their minds to always focus on the possibilities instead of the obstacles. Successful people think Big, and then they make very wise choices. Because when it comes right down to it, success is a choice.

> **"All out dreams can come true if we have the courage to pursue them."**
>
> *Walt Disney*

You can learn to think and act like successful people do. Once you start thinking big, you'll start succeeding big, and that's what I want to help you do with this book.

As you read this book, I'll be hitting you with success principles from all different directions. Sometimes I'll repeat the timeless principles of success in order to help condition your subconscious mind to buy into these ideas and to begin acting on them.

If you consistently and persistently apply the principles in this book, before long you'll be able to write your own success story.

I was never a great athlete. In fact, I was always the last kid picked for sports in school. But I used the principles in this book to go from being a bench-warmer in my college soccer team to an Olympic athlete only four years later. After my Olympic career, I used these same principles to build several successful businesses. If these principles worked for me, they will work for you.

This book is broken down into seven parts. Part One is about the dream—how to find your dream and purpose in life. In Part Two you will learn how to get yourself to take consistent and persistent action in the pursuit of your dream. Part Three reveals how to create a flawless plan and how to set goals. In Part Four, you'll learn how to become a better leader so you can create a dream team that will help you realize your goals and dreams. Part Five will show you how to become committed to your mission. Part Six will show you how to overcome the inevitable challenges you will face. Finally, in Part Seven, you'll learn how to become all that you can be in the pursuit of your goals.

Once you start winning battles on the way to your dream, do me a favor. Shoot me an email and share your victories with me. Your victories will fuel my victories.

Ruben Gonzalez — Ruben@thelugeman.com
TheOlympicSpeaker.com

" Those who dream by night
in the dusty recesses of their minds
wake in the morning to find
that all was vanity;
but the dreamers of the day
are dangerous...
for they may act on their dream...
and make it possible. "

— T.E. Lawrence, *Seven Pillars of Wisdom*

"Life is either a daring adventure or nothing.

— Helen Keller"

PART I
THE DREAM

Warming the bench on my college soccer team.

> **Man is only truly great when he acts from his passion.**
>
> — Benjamin Disraeli

You Were Created for Greatness

For the last 30 years, I have been a student of success. During that time, I've read hundreds of biographies and manuscripts in search of the timeless principles of success. After studying the lives of the most successful people in history, people like Thomas Edison, Abraham Lincoln, George Washington, Thomas Jefferson, the Wright Brothers, Mother Theresa, Martin Luther King and countless others, I discovered a secret that changed my life. A secret so empowering, so powerful, that anyone who embraces it can use it to realize their fondest hopes and dreams. A secret that you can use today to create a better future.

Are you ready to discover the secret? Well here it is… Great people were not born great. They became great by making a **decision** to pursue their dream in life and by refusing to give up. The struggle they faced on the road to their dreams is what made them great. The struggle forced them to dig down deep inside themselves. Only when they dug down deep inside, did they find their gifts.

> **"There is greatness within you."**

You have God-given greatness within you. Your greatness will be revealed as you pursue your dream. And you will accomplish extraordinary things if you consistently and persistently follow the principles of success laid out in this book. These are the same principles I learned from studying the greatest people in history.

You can learn to unlock your special powers to attract whatever you want in your life. It's just a skill. Give yourself a chance to learn the fundamental skills that lead to success, and you will hold the power to create your own future.

Put It into Action:

Learn the principles of success and use them to propel yourself to victory.

The Power of
What You Say

Successful people understand that even though we might be programmed for mediocrity, we were designed and created for extraordinary achievement.

Conditioning our minds for extraordinary achievement is simple, but not easy. The road to huge successes in all areas of your life can be broken down into five steps:

1) **What you say to yourself**
2) **Your beliefs and thoughts**
3) **What you do**
4) **Your daily habits**
5) **Your results**

What you tell yourself influences what your beliefs and thoughts are. Your thoughts determine what you do. What you do repeatedly becomes your habits. Your habits determine your results. If you are not happy with your results, change what you say to yourself and surround yourself with people who support and encourage the quest for your dream. If you do that, before long you'll start getting different results.

> **You get and become what you think and talk about most.**

Successful people constantly talk about and think about what they want. Unsuccessful people constantly talk about and think about what they don't want.

How about you? What do you constantly think about? What do you always talk about? Is it what you want or what you don't want? How about the people you spend most of your time with? Are they focusing on dreams or on nightmares? Are they mentors or are they tor-mentors?

Did you know your income is the average income of the people you spend most of your time with? Want to double your income? Start hanging around people who make twice what you're making. You'll start thinking big, acting big, and earning big. Seriously!

Put It Into Action:

Start talking and thinking about what you want to accomplish in your life. Associate with successful people to become more successful. Find a coach or mentor who will help you accelerate your success.

It All Starts With Belief

The first step in high achievement is in believing that success is possible. When I was ten years old and began dreaming of competing in the Olympics, I did not think it was a possible dream. After all, I was not a great athlete and was always the last kid picked to play sports in P.E.

I needed to start believing in myself in order to get myself to take action. Lack of self-belief or lack of confidence results in fear of failure, and **that's** what keeps people from pursuing their dreams. After all, if you don't believe you can achieve your dream, why even try?

Belief is the driving force—the power behind all great accomplishments. Believing that something is possible leads to looking for ways to make it possible. The how-to-do-it comes to the person who believes he can do it. When you believe, you'll attract helpers, because all of a sudden your confidence shows, so others start believing in you. Once you believe, you'll be ready to commit to taking action. And, believe me, success requires taking **massive action** – for a long time. Unless you commit, you'll never make your dream come true.

There are a couple of things you can do to raise your self belief level. The books you read and the people you associate with will ultimately determine what you believe. Let's talk about reading the right books.

> **Belief is the driving force behind achievement.**

My dad always encouraged me to read biographies. Dad said, "Ruben, why don't you read some biographies – the stories of great people? If you read about the lives of people you look up to, people you admire, you'll learn what works and what doesn't work in life, because success leaves clues." Then, he backed off and let the books work their magic.

I began reading biographies and started loving them. I read tons of them. My favorites were the stories of people who had overcome great odds to realize their dreams. Before long, I realized that ordinary people could accomplish the extraordinary if they consistently followed success principles.

If you don't like to read, tune in to the Biography Channel and, before long, you'll start to believe, too!

Put It Into Action:

Read biographies of people who overcame great odds to realize their dreams. Tune in to The Biography Channel. Learn how to be more successful from someone who is already successful. Find a mentor or coach.

How To Fuel
Your Desire To Win

There are many facets to success. You have to have a dream—something you're shooting for. You have to believe in yourself. You have to take massive action with an attitude that you are willing to do whatever it takes for as long as it takes. Then, and only then, is success realistic.

More than anything else, your desire will determine if you'll make it. How bad do you want it? Is your dream something that you'd like to do? Is it something that would be nice to do? Or is it something that you are obsessed about?

How badly you want it will determine whether you'll realize your dream, because how bad you want it determines what will make you quit. Burning desire allows a person with average ability to successfully compete with those who have far more ability. Desire allows you to give it everything you've got. It helps you reach your full potential. Intense desire allows people to win against overwhelming odds.

If your dream is not an obsession, as soon as you come across obstacles, you'll quit. As soon as the challenge of reaching your dream becomes an inconvenience, you'll give up. Success is not convenient. Trust me. In order to succeed, you will need to inconvenience yourself in a big way—for a long time. That's why it's so important to be driven, excited, and passionate about your dream. If your "why?" is big enough, the "how" will take care of itself.

To succeed, you need to know how to feed your desire. The more you feed your desire, the harder it is to quit. Most of the mental training we do as Olympic athletes is designed to do two things—strengthen our belief level and fuel our desire. How do you do that? How do you turn your dream into a magnificent obsession?

You surround yourself with the dream. You put pictures of your dream all around you. The walls in my office are completely covered with Olympic memorabilia. By surrounding myself with the dream, all day long I'm bombarding my mind with where I want to go. If I daydream, I daydream Olympics.

I talk to everyone about my dream. I think about my dream all day long, and I dream about my dream all night long. I vividly imagine what it's going to feel like when I'm walking into the Opening Ceremonies. You can watch a video where I talk about the visualization process at TheOlympicSpeaker.com.

Writing about your dream is also a powerful exercise because writing your dreams and goals is an act of commitment that becomes ingrained in your subconscious mind. Whenever you put your thoughts down on paper, your mind gets very focused and intense.

Do the same with **your** dream. Get obsessed! Get focused! And, make it happen!

Put It Into Action:

Get pictures of your dream. Talk about it. Visualize it. Surround yourself with like-minded people. And then, take massive action!

Use Your Strengths

Have you ever been in a situation where work seemed effortless? Well, you were probably in a situation that required you to use your personal strengths.

Socrates said, "Know thyself." Socrates was right on the money. Knowing your strengths and weaknesses makes your success journey faster and easier. The better you understand what your strengths are, the better equipped you will be to find an arena you are suited to play in and then come up with a strategy that will help you win in that arena.

This concept applies in sports, in education, at home, and in your personal and professional success.

Successful people focus on their strengths. Do you know yours?

In sports, knowing yourself is not as complicated. Your body type rules out many sports. Someone built like a linebacker will not make an effective wide receiver. I would not make a good sumo wrestler *or* a good jockey.

If I hadn't known what my strengths were, I never would have made it to the Olympics. As I tell my audiences, I was not a great athlete. My main strength was perseverance. I chose the sport of luge because I knew I could persevere in the face of challenges. I figured the luge was so dangerous that there would be many quitters.

My strategy was to outlast the competition. I never would have been able to come up with an effective strategy if I had not known what my strengths were.

A few years ago, I took a personality assessment test.

> **Successful people focus on their strengths.**

The report was uncanny. It revealed things about me that I did not consciously know, but once I read them, I immediately agreed with. The report gave me insights about myself that have helped me build my businesses and also helped me whenever I communicate with others – my wife, my children, my colleagues, my prospects, etc.

I've always worked hard. The knowledge from this report allows me to work smart, as well. Bottom line, it made me more productive. It gives me an edge. It helps me win more in life and at work. If you want to be more successful, discover your strengths and focus on your strengths.

Put It Into Action:

Take a personality test. You'll be glad you did. I personally recommend the DISC and Kolbe tests. They are terrific. Once you discover your strengths, focus on them and team up with people who are strong in the areas where you are weak.

Find Your
Dream And Purpose

Benjamin Franklin said, "Most men die at age 25 but are not buried until they are 70." What he meant was, most people give up on their dreams before they are 30 years old and spend the rest of their lives in "survival mode," living day to day, just trying to get through the day rather than living a life filled with passion, in the pursuit of their dreams.

Unless you are crystal-clear about your life purpose, mission, calling, or destiny, and unless you believe it is possible for you to make your dream a reality, you will not act on it and you'll revert to "survival mode." Believe me, "survival mode" is not a good place to be.

You were created to realize your dream. It is your life purpose. It is your calling. It's your mission. Your dream will draw on your God-given talent; it will appeal to your highest ideals and will give you unlimited energy. Having a dream connects with the spirit that dwells in our heart; it gives us an outlet for our unique gifts and talents and makes us feel that our lives matter. It makes us feel that we are making a difference.

A powerful dream gives you a future focus. Instead of being worried about the frustrations of the present, a dream gets you thinking about the possibilities of the future. A dream gives you energy. Finally, a dream keeps you from wasting your life. Dreams keep you from wasting your talents, abilities, and creativity. They keep you from living a life filled with regret and that terrible, "What might have been?" feeling.

You will experience success in life to the extent that you are clear about and commit to achieving your life purpose.

The experiences you have had up to this point in your life have prepared you for your life purpose. You have unique talents, abilities, interests, and values that only you can bring to greatness. There is a destiny that only you can fulfill. But, first, you need to find out what you would love to do—what you would be willing to do for free. Figure out what you are good at doing. Know what is extremely important to you. Discover what you were born to do.

> **"Dedicate your life to the pursuit of your dream."**

What are your greatest talents? What do others say you are good at? What have your unique life experiences prepared you to do? What do you love to do so much that you would do it for free?

Remember, you can't make your dream come true if you don't even know what it is. If you can't see it, you can't get it. Once you see it, dedicate your life to making it a reality. Give yourself to your vision. You are worthy of it. It's why you're here. It's how you will make a difference in the world. It's how you'll be remembered. It's your legacy.

Put It Into Action:

Take some quality time to think about your dreams and your natural talents and spend the rest of your life pursuing your dreams.

66 **Dream as if you'll live forever.**
Live as if you'll die today. 99

— James Dean

> **If one advances confidently in the direction of his dreams, he will meet with a success unexpected in common hours.**

— Henry David Thoreau

PART II
TAKING ACTION

Learning the basics of luge in Lake Placid, 1984.

**" Thinking will not
overcome fear but action will. "**

— W. Clement Stone

The Power of a Team

In November of 2006, my good friend Greg Reid and I were talking about how there ought to be a movie about how to become more successful in life—an entertaining movie that taught people of all ages the universal success principles that work for anyone, anywhere, anytime.

At the time, neither Greg nor I had any experience making movies. But, that didn't matter. We were excited about the idea and committed to make it happen.

Only two weeks later, Greg had found a Hollywood studio, a director, producer, camera crews, editors, music people—the works. You see, it doesn't matter if you have the knowledge to realize your dream. If you do, that's great. If you don't, you simply create a team made up of people who do have the knowledge.

We had the movie production people in place. Now, we had to find the most successful people in America to interview. We started hitting the phones. At first, nobody wanted to be involved, but we kept on making calls. Winston Churchill said, "If you're going through hell, keep going!"

We kept making the calls. Then, all of a sudden, we started finding CEOs, best-selling authors, top speakers, inventors, and athletes. After a while, people stared calling us, asking to be in the movie. You see, the law of attraction works best if you put it in action. It's the **action** behind the attraction that makes dreams come true.

> **Create a team and bring your dream to life.**

Our movie is called "Pass It On." It's about learning the principles of success, applying them in your own life, and then passing them on to others.

"Pass It On" was featured in the Sundance Film Festival, it had the biggest movie premiere in Las Vegas history, and is quickly becoming the most popular movie in its genre. Not bad for a couple of guys who can't even run a video camera! You can get your own copy at TheOlympicSpeaker.com.

Remember, if the "why" is big enough, the "how" will take care of itself. If you are committed to your dream and willing to do the work, it doesn't matter if you have all the knowledge and resources. Create a team of committed people who do have the resources and the knowledge and bring your dream to life! And, remember... it's the action behind the attraction that makes dreams come true!

Put It Into Action:

Get committed to your dream. Then, use your excitement to attract people to your team. Create a dream team and make your fondest dreams a reality.

Acting in Spite of Your Fear

When I first watched the Olympics as a kid, what impressed me the most about the Olympians was not their athletic ability. What I admired about the Olympians was their spirit. You see, these were people who had a dream and the courage to fully commit to it for years with no guarantee of success.

Sure, they had outstanding athletic ability. But more importantly, they had the faith, the guts, the boldness, and the willingness to go for it with no guarantees of success. They had that rare attitude of not worrying about the possibility of failure. They were going to go for it and commit 100% to winning, no matter what. It's like they said to themselves, "It's my dream, and I'm going for it. That's it, period!"

When you move boldly toward your goals, when you make the decision to do whatever it takes, magic happens. All of a sudden, unseen forces will come to your aid. The bolder and more committed you become, the more your subconscious will work for you. You will unconsciously start to attract the people and resources you need to achieve your goal.

When you are focused on your goal, your mind starts acting like a guided missile. It becomes tuned into anything that might help you achieve your goal. That's why it is said that fortune favors the brave and that boldness has magic in it.

People will start saying that you are lucky. Winners know there is no such thing as luck. All that is really happening is that you have now become driven. You are known for your goal. Everybody can see it. Your every action is broadcasting to the world where you are headed, and all of a sudden, anyone who might be interested in helping you can see you are serious.

> **"Courage is acting in spite of your fear."**

When you put all of your energy into one goal, you tap into huge resources. That single decision changes everything. All the stress and worry disappear. Your mental attitude changes completely as you are transformed into the hunter, while the dream has become the prey that will eventually succumb to you.

When you make the decision to commit 100%, the winner inside you comes out. The champion inside you emerges. The real you comes out. You just have to have the courage to face your fears and pursue your dream.

Put it into action:

Make a quality decision that failure is not an option and that you will take bold action in the pursuit of your goals and dreams. Find a coach or mentor who will help you reach your goals in record time.

Fortune Favors the Brave

Your fears are a smokescreen. They are like ghosts that keep you from being your best. It's okay to be afraid. Everyone is afraid! What's **not** okay is to let your fears get the best of you. Successful people have learned to act in spite of their fears. And that's what courage is – acting in spite of your fears.

Courage can be developed. Aristotle said, "You become what you repeatedly do." The way to develop courage is by practicing courage in every situation where courage is required. How do you do that? Through a quality decision. You come to the realization that whenever you are afraid to do something, you are simply being tested. You make a decision that from now on you will win over your fear. Remember; if you do what you fear, the fear will disappear. If you don't do what you fear, the fear will control your life.

Make a game out of conquering your fears. You can get started with small things. For example, if you usually wait to hear what everyone else orders when you're at a restaurant, next time, be the first to order. By doing that, you'll experience a small personal victory. You just won over that fear. The next time you're talking to somebody and want to ask a question but are afraid of looking stupid, ask anyway. Guess what? You've just won another personal victory. Score: Fears – 0, Courage –2.

> **You become what you repeatedly do.**

You need to win many personal victories before you will win a public victory. By becoming conscious of your fears and making a game out of conquering them, before long, in your heart, you'll begin to understand that fears are just smokescreens. By playing that game all the time, you become more and more courageous every day.

Put It Into Action:

Make a game out of staring fear in the face. Start doing what you fear and watch your fear disappear. Start chalking up some personal victories so you can start experiencing some public victories.

Get Started
and Don't Quit

There are two parts of courage that lead to success. The first part is the willingness to begin, to act in faith, to step out boldly in the direction of your goals, even if there is no guarantee of success. The second part of courage is the willingness to endure, to persist, to refuse to give up, and to keep on working harder than anyone else.

Most people talk themselves out of going for their dream before they try. Most of the ones who make the attempt quit as soon as the going gets tough. It's so sad because **everyone** has the ability to make their dreams come true. It's sad that so few people have the willingness to do what it takes.

That's why we root for the underdog. That's why we love movies like "Rocky" and "Rudy." We love hearing those stories because all of us have felt like the underdog at one time or another. Seeing the underdog win gives us hope that we can win, too.

Once you get started on the road to making your dreams a reality, you must make the decision to never quit. The decision to never give up gives you a huge advantage because the person who is most determined usually wins.

A study on goals and perseverance found that 95% of the goals that people set are ultimately achieved—as long as the person didn't give up. Ninety-five percent! That's almost a guarantee that if you refuse to quit, you will eventually win. The main reason people fail isn't because of lack of ability or opportunities. They fail because they lack the inner strength to persist in the face of obstacles and difficulties.

Don't worry about failing. Failing is how you learn. You can fail over and over again, but all it takes is one big success to wipe out all

> # "Fortune favors the brave. Boldness has magic in it."

your previous failures. The only time you can't afford to fail is the last time you try. The more you persist, the more you will believe in yourself. And the more you believe in yourself, the more you persist. Your persistence is a measure of how much you believe in yourself and how much you believe in your ability to succeed. If you act as if you are guaranteed to succeed, your belief will grow. That's because emotion follows motion. What you do determines how you will feel. Act in spite of your fears and commit to not quit, and I promise that the winner inside you will burst forth to propel you to victory.

Put It Into Action:

Start stepping out in faith. Stop waiting until everything is perfect before taking action. Find an accountability partner who will encourage you to pursue your dreams. Do what every Olympic athlete does to be their best, and find a coach or mentor who will encourage you and push you to be your best.

How To Get Yourself
To Take Action

How do you find the strength to keep doing what you know you need to do day after day, after day, after day? How do you get yourself to consistently do what you know you need to be doing?

Like anything else, it's all a mental game. The best way to win a mental battle is by using everything in your arsenal at once. Do a variety of things to get you to perform like you know you should. Successful people use all of the following techniques...

1. **Constantly focus on the dream. Focus on what drives you to take action.**

2. **Write your goals down and read them daily.**

3. **Constantly visualize how great it will feel when you reach your goal (to get your desire for gain working for you).**

4. **Use positive affirmations whenever a negative thought enters your mind.**

5. Share your goal with people who support you to build pressure.

6. Find a coach or accountability partner who will hold your feet to the fire and get you to do what you won't do on your own.

You need to fight it on all fronts. Develop the habit of controlling your thoughts, or your thoughts will control you!

Put It Into Action:

Make a decision that you will do whatever it takes to get yourself to take consistent and persistent action towards your dreams and goals. In success, action is where the rubber meets the road. Find a coach or mentor who will push you to be your best.

No Guts No Glory

You know in your heart what you'd like to accomplish. You're always thinking about it. It bugs you all the time. Just the thought of doing it makes your skin tingle. The thought of finally making that dream a reality makes you feel alive, excited, and pumped up with a terrific feeling of anticipation.

But, something is holding you back. What if you go for it and you fail? How could you live with yourself? What would others think? Fear of failure holds most people back from going after their dreams. With every day that you hesitate, the fear grows stronger.

The fear is just a smokescreen! I dare you to act in spite of your fears. You'll be so glad you did. Regardless of the results, you will feel so proud of yourself! And even if you do fail (which only means you need to try a different approach), others will look up to you for having the guts to act with courage.

Go for it! Just going for it will put you in the top 5% of the population. Why? Because 95% of the people out there are afraid to pursue their dreams.

The one quality that separates the most successful people from the least is initiative. Initiative means taking responsibility and taking action when you see something needs to be done. It means moving quickly and decisively.

Initiative means taking risks, regularly moving out of the comfort zone, and doing things the average person is not willing to do. You can do it. You have it in you. You really do. I know. I know because **I'm** an average person who was able to accomplish some amazing things only because I was constantly willing to dive headfirst out of my comfort zone.

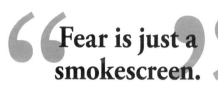
Fear is just a smokescreen.

Believe me, when you fully commit to your dream and start acting boldly in its pursuit, the world will **conspire** to help your dreams become a reality.

Do you have the guts to go for it? If you're reading this, I believe you do. Just go for it!

Put It Into Action:

Imagine how dreadful your life will be if you don't go for your dream…Imagine what an adventure your life will be if you dedicate it to the pursuit of your dreams. When your grandchildren ask you what you did with your life, will you tell them you played it safe, or will you enthrall them with the stories of your adventures? Find a coach or mentor who will help you make your life magnificent.

Take a Chance

The most successful people in the world are risk takers. As soon as they see an opportunity, they move quickly and make something happen. They have a special quality that sets them apart from less successful people. They take initiative in everything they do. Successful people accept responsibility and take action when they see something needs to be done. They don't suffer from paralysis of analysis. They just do something—**anything** that will get them closer to their goal.

By taking action—massive action, they build momentum and soon good things start to happen. My business coach likes to say, "Most people need to think less and act more." One of my other mentors always says, "Done is better than perfect." Another way to say it is – implement now, perfect later. If you want to succeed, be willing to fail. To succeed big, be willing to fail big. To succeed fast, be willing to fail fast.

Successful people are willing to try different approaches to reach their goal. They aren't worried about failing. They are focused only on the result. They just throw mud on the wall, knowing that if they throw enough, some of it will stick. They never focus on the approaches that didn't work. There's no time for that. Wallowing with self pity is for losers. Winners simply learn from their mistakes and **quickly** try a different approach.

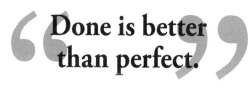

" **Done is better than perfect.** "

The faster they move, the more energy they have. The more different things they try, the more likely they are to succeed. They make a game out of it, and they never take their focus away from the goal. Their attitude is – there is always a way. I will find a way. I will succeed.

A national survey of octogenarians revealed that their biggest regret in life was not taking enough risks. Think about that! What they're saying is they realize they didn't live life to the fullest and they missed out. When you turn 80, you don't want to have that regret. So, go for it. Take a chance. Do something—you'll be glad you did.

Put It Into Action:

Are you going to go for it or not? If you're not, why don't you just give this book to someone who will use it? Are you mad yet? I hope so. Most people don't do anything until they get mad! But, don't waste your anger on me. Instead, use your anger to pursue your dream. Passion is positive anger. Stop analyzing everything. Think less and act more. Remember, you are worthy of your dream.

" A good plan violently executed now is better than a perfect plan executed next week. "

— George S. Patton

**" A man owes very little
to what he is born with — a man
is what he makes of himself. "**

— Alexander Graham Bell

PART III
SETTING GOALS &
PLANNING AHEAD

End of luge run Lake Placid, 1984.

> **" A goal without a plan is just a wish. "**

— Ruben Gonzalez

Successful People
Set Goals

The most successful people in the world are extremely goal oriented. They know **exactly** what they want, and they are always focused on achieving it.

Goals keep you focused, and they help you to be more confident and motivated. Goals keep you from drifting through life with no purpose.

The main difference between successful people and unsuccessful people is how they think. Successful people think about what they want and how to get it. Unsuccessful people think and talk about what they don't want. Setting goals helps you to keep thinking about where you want to go.

People who set goals live more meaningful and purposeful lives. They are more in control of their destiny and therefore happier. People are happier when they are doing something that is moving them toward something they want. Goal setting is so powerful that I'll bet just the thought of achieving your goals puts a smile on your face.

Your goals need to be crystal-clear, written, and **very** specific. They also need to be measurable. You have to know when you have achieved them.

Write your goals down every day. It only takes a couple of minutes. Make it a rule that you can't turn on your computer until you've written your goals down. I challenge you to do this! And I guarantee you that if you do it for a year, your life will change dramatically!

"Goals keep you focused."

Talk about your goals to other people. See if you can get them to write *their* goals. It's a great way to impact other people's lives. And remember to focus on **why** you have those goals. The "why" is the driving force.

Once you start writing your goals, talking about your goals, and thinking about your goals, you will start turning into a success-seeking guided missile that won't miss.

Put It Into Action:

What do you want to be? What do you want to do? What do you want to have? Write those goals down. But don't just write them, take action. What can you do in the next 15 minutes that will help you get closer to your goals? DO IT…NOW! Find a coach or mentor who will keep you accountable to your goals.

How To Set Goals
Like A Champion

There are four basic steps that will help you make the most of goal setting. First, choose a goal; next, see yourself succeeding at your goal. After that, choose a quality that will help you achieve your goal, and finally, create a new habit that will help propel you toward accomplishing your goal.

What changes would you like to make in your life that excite you just by thinking about them? What would you love to do? Where do you want to be 10 years from now? What is your dream? Knowing those answers is good, but just thinking about your goal is not enough. If you want to reach your goal, you need to make it real—write it down! Don't worry how you'll make your dream come true at first. Magic happens when you put your goals down on paper. Writing it down is the first step in turning a dream you might achieve into a goal you will achieve.

Several times a day, close your eyes and for a couple minutes vividly imagine what it's going to feel like when you achieve your goal. Really get into it. Feel it as if it were really happening–right now! Get excited! Your subconscious does not know the difference between imagining it and it really happening. By doing this, you become passionate about your desire, your belief becomes unshakeable, and you become unstoppable. You mentally go from "wishful thinking" to "belief." You can see an example of me going through this visualization exercise by visiting TheOlympicSpeaker.com and watching the demo video. You'll learn how I visualized myself walking into the Olympic stadium during the Opening Ceremony.

> **"Magic happens when you put your goals down on paper."**

The third step in reaching your goal is to choose the main quality you think you'll need to reach your goal. Is it Boldness? Creativity? Enthusiasm? Patience? Leadership? In my case, it was Perseverance. To become good at the luge, I knew I was going to have to endure many crashes and injuries and simply refuse to give up. So, I made a decision to become perseverant. Someone said, "The main difference between a successful person and a failure is that the successful person tried one more time." I decided to persevere by always trying one more time.

Finally, you need to create a new habit that will help you achieve your goal. Good habits don't usually just happen. You need to develop a specific plan for creating a new habit. It's simply a matter of choosing an action that helps develop your quality, deciding when to practice that habit, knowing that you are going to have to repeat it many times, and then giving yourself a reminder.

Since perseverance was the most important quality I needed to reach my goal, it was necessary for me to find ways to develop my perseverance. I had to get good at "not quitting." So, I decided to become an expert on perseverance. I read books about people who had faced great challenges and refused to give up. I got inspired that if they could – I could! I made a decision that no matter how bad a crash I had, I would get back on my sled. I had a picture of a luge athlete riding a sled, and I used that picture to remind me to get back on my sled.

By following these four steps, I was able to turn my goals into habits that ultimately helped me realize my dream. If you commit to these four steps, you will be able to realize your dreams and goals, as well.

Put It Into Action:

What is your goal? Close your eyes and vividly imagine what it will feel like, taste like, smell like, and look like when you realize your goal. DO IT…NOW! What quality do you need to develop to realize your goal? What new habit will you develop to reach your goal? Now, persistently and consistently take the actions that will get you to your destination.

People tend to overestimate what they can do in one year and underestimate what they can accomplish in five years. When you set your five year goals, you need to make sure they are huge goals—goals that will take your breath away.

"Whatever you vividly imagine, ardently desire, sincerely believe, and enthusiastically act upon... must eventually come to pass!"

— Paul J. Meyer

The First Step
In Your Journey

Imagine that you are about to drive your family on a cross-country trip from Los Angeles to New York City.

Your first step would be to determine exactly where you were and where you wanted to go. Then, you would get an appropriate map (a map of Europe would not do) and you would plan your route.

If you encountered road blocks once you were en route, you would make detours and take alternate routes, but your final destination, NYC, would not change.

Life is very similar to taking a family road trip.

You decide where you want to go, you determine exactly where you are, and you make a plan. Your plan is flexible because it must take into account unforeseen circumstances, but your destination is fixed.

Another way of saying it is "You write your plans in sand, but you write your dreams and goals in concrete."

An airplane pilot flying from Los Angeles to New York does the same thing. Ninety-nine percent of the time he is off course (the wind keeps blowing him off course), but he does not get discouraged. He simply keeps making course corrections in order to reach his destination.

Even on final approach, the pilot is making hundreds of tiny course corrections in order to land the plane safely on the runway's center stripe.

You must be brutally honest about where you are when you get started. Otherwise, the best plans will not help you. You must do a skills inventory in order to know your strengths and weaknesses. It's important to know your weaknesses in order to know where you might need help.

Ask yourself: How did I get to my current situation? What did I do right? What could I have done differently?

You can always learn from the past. You want to extract all the lessons you can from the past in order to be better prepared for the future.

Now that you know where you are and where you want to go, the next question you need to ask yourself is: What do I need to do to get from where I am to where I want to go?

And....What should I stop doing? Who should I be spending more time with? What activities or people are holding me back?

By taking the time to analyze where you are, where you want to go, and how you will get there, you will save months, or even years, on your journey.

Put It Into Action:

Ask yourself the critical questions that will help you develop a plan of action. Where are you now? Where do you want to go? What resources do you need? What do you need to do to get where you want to go? Then, take action and expect to have to adjust your plans.

Focus, You Won't Succeed Without It

Being focused is not an option if you are serious about realizing your dreams. Being focused on your dream is critical to making it become a reality.

Back in 1984, when I made a decision to take up the sport of luge and make a run at the Olympics, I took an 8 x 10 photo of a luge racer and hung it on the wall across from my bed. The first thing I saw every morning was "The Luge Man." He reminded me to work out, eat right and surround myself with winners. The last thing I saw every night before I turned off the lights was "The Luge Man." All night long I would dream about the luge and about the Olympics.

I never met "The Luge Man," but he is one of my heroes. He helped keep me focused on my objective. And he was a factor that helped make my dream come true.

I'm not the only person whose dream was focused by a photograph. The Great Depression was not kind to (legendary Hotelier) Conrad Hilton. After the crash of 1929, people weren't traveling, and if they were, they weren't staying in the hotels Hilton had acquired during the boom years of the 1920s.

By 1931, his creditors were threatening to foreclose, his laundry was in hock, and he was borrowing money from a bellboy so he could eat. That year, Hilton came across a photograph of the Waldorf Hotel with its six kitchens, 200 cooks, 500 waiters, 2,000 rooms, and its private hospital and private railroad siding in the basement. Hilton clipped the photograph out of the magazine and wrote across it, "The Greatest of Them All."

The year 1931 was "a presumptuous, an outrageous time to dream," Hilton later wrote. But he put the photo of the Waldorf in his wallet, and when he had a desk again, slipped the picture under the glass top. From that moment on, it was always in front of him. As he worked his way back up and acquired new, bigger desks, he continued to slip the cherished photo under the glass. Eighteen years later, in October 1949, Conrad Hilton acquired the Waldorf.

That picture gave Hilton's dream shape and substance. There was something for his mind to focus upon. It became a cue for his behavior.

How focused are you on achieving your goal? Is it an obsession? Do you write your goal every day? You need to. Writing your goal daily is an act of commitment that slowly turns you into a guided missile that can't miss.

Do you surround yourself with pictures of your goal? If your goal is to drive a Mercedes, do you regularly test-drive a Mercedes? Do you subscribe to Mercedes Magazine? You need to.

Put It Into Action:

Surround yourself with pictures of your goals and dreams. Vividly imagine what it will be like when you finally realize your goals and dreams. And, be patient. Give yourself time. Remember, Hilton acquired the Waldorf 18 years later, not 18 months later!

Feedback –
The Breakfast Of Champions

There is a simple thing you can start doing right now to help you improve everything in your life. It's something that doesn't take much time, but saves you huge amounts of time. That something is asking for feedback from qualified people - from a coach.

As soon as we step off our sled at the end of each luge run, we immediately pick up the walkie-talkie to talk to coach.

Notice we don't call the track workers or the fans along the track to ask for feedback. They just saw our luge run, but all they saw was a body hurling down a chute of ice. The track workers and the fans are not qualified to give us quality feedback. Coach is. Coach is qualified because he was the World Champion three times and because he sees things we cannot see. As we're zooming by at almost 90 MPH three feet away from him, Coach's trained eye sees minute things that can help us make quick improvements.

Coach might say, "Ruben, you were too late into curve six. When you entered the curve, you were five inches from the left wall. You need to be two inches from the wall. You had a small dip in the middle of the curve. Try holding it up in the middle. You tapped your left foot when you exited the curve. You need to relax and trust the sled. Finally, it seemed like your right shoulder was hunched up. Make sure you settle into the sled more carefully at the

start so your poor position will not torque you down the track."
Coach sees all the mistakes and tells me how to improve.

Later that day, after dinner, we all watch videos of our runs so we can see for ourselves what coach saw. That night, we think about the day's feedback, and we formulate a plan to be better tomorrow.

You need to do the same thing in all aspects of your life. Find qualified people to give you quality feedback so you can constantly improve all areas of your life—so you can make your life a masterpiece. Find a mentor, a life coach, or a business coach who will help you accelerate your success.

Most people won't volunteer feedback, so you have to ask for it. There are several ways to ask for feedback. You could ask someone, "How do you see me limiting myself?," "What else could I do to improve?," or "On a scale of 1 to 10, how would you rate my report? My work over the last quarter? My communication skills?"

If the answer is less than a perfect 10, ask, "What would it take to make it a 10?" That's important information. It's specific information that will help you improve.

Most people are afraid of asking for feedback. They shouldn't be. They are better off knowing the truth. Once you know the truth, you can do something about it. What if I was too proud to pick up the walkie-talkie? I might believe my luge run was a 10 when it really was a 7. Then, I would continue making the same mistakes. I'd never improve.

After someone gives you feedback, thank them. Let them know you appreciate them for caring enough about you to share that information. Once you get the feedback, apply it in route to your goal and watch your progress accelerate

Put it into action:

Ask for feedback from qualified people. Thank them. Then, take immediate action with your new information.

Measuring Your Progress

As you set goals and begin working toward them, it is critical that you establish benchmarks you can use to evaluate your progress. The more specific your measures are, the faster you'll reach your goals because you'll reduce wasted time.

Your subconscious mind works best when you set clear goals with deadlines. When you do, your subconscious mind will act like an autopilot that will steer you toward your goals. It will act like a radar that is tuned into finding anything that might help you reach your goals.

It is important to identify all of the tasks you need to do to reach your goal. Once you have identified the tasks, you should prioritize them and focus on the most important task first.

You may have to break down each task into smaller sub-tasks— and so on. Each sub-task should have its own deadline. Deadlines create urgency and compel you to take action. For example, imagine that in the next seven years, you wanted to climb the highest mountains in each of the seven continents, known as the Seven Peaks. You would have to learn all about mountaineering, find guides, determine the best order to climb them, and focus on the first task - climbing Mt. Kilimanjaro.

Climbing Mt. Kili would then be broken down into sub-tasks: Getting into incredible physical shape, financing the expedition, acquiring know-how, finding guides, purchasing climbing gear, etc.

Each of those sub-tasks might be broken down even further. For example, in order to become fit enough to climb, you might have to change your diet, train yourself like a marathoner, lose 30 lbs, etc.

What you're doing is starting with the deadline and working backwards to see when all the other steps must be completed. If you don't set deadlines, by human nature, you never do what you need to do to accomplish the goal.

Once you set deadlines and start taking action, you'll be amazed at how great you feel as you check off completed tasks. Before long, you start creating momentum; and when momentum is on your side, everything in the process will seem more and more effortless and fun.

Along the way, you should keep careful records and measure your progress because what cannot be measured cannot be managed.

No matter what your goal is, you can focus on smaller tasks that can be measured to gauge your progress. If you want to improve your sales, you could focus on how many calls you make each day. If you'd like a promotion, you could ask your boss for specific tasks you could focus on to make yourself more valuable. If you want to improve your relationships, you could focus on how many minutes you spend with that special person.

Put It Into Action:

To create momentum, break your goals down into smaller measurable tasks and tackle them one at a time. Keep good records and measure your progress.

Game Plans For Success

Everyone wants to win. Wanting to win is not enough. You have to be willing to prepare to win. No matter how many times we've been to a particular luge track, before we train on it, we "walk the track" with Coach.

A typical week during the luge World Cup circuit is like this: Tuesday through Friday, we take our training and qualifying runs; Saturday and Sunday, we race; and Mondays are for traveling to the next track.

Within Europe, we drive in vans from track to track. For races outside of Europe, we fly. No matter how long we've been traveling, no matter how tired we are, whether we've just ridden in a van for twelve hours from Innsbruck to Sarajevo or flown ten hours from Europe to Calgary, before we go to the hotel, we walk the track.

We go to the top of the track, and for two hours, we literally walk down the track, slipping and sliding the whole way, planning exactly what lines we will take during training. Coach knows the best lines—he was World Champion three times. Coach knows the shortcut to success. We follow Coach and take detailed notes on everything he says.

Typically, it goes something like this; "Okay, guys, this is curve three. You want to enter early. At this point, you want to be no more than three inches from the left wall. Over here, steer with a force of three (where zero is no steering and ten is all you've got). Down there at the expansion joint, give it a five; over there by that sign, hold it up; then at the end, crank it with all you've got but remember to counter steer or else you'll slam into the wall."

We feverishly write every word he says. Some of us even record Coach as he's talking. When we finally get to the hotel, we don't go straight to bed; we memorize the fastest lines and start visualizing our perfect run.

What if, on the way to the track I had told Coach, "Coach, I'm not feeling well. Will you just drop me off at the hotel?"

You know what would happen? I'd take a hot shower, get a hot meal, snuggle under the warm covers, watch "Friends" or "Frazier" on TV in Serbo-Croatian while sipping a hot chocolate, and drift into a wonderful night's sleep. All the while, I'd be thinking, "Those fools! They're freezing their rear ends out there!" Then the next day, I'd kill myself on the track and have only myself to blame.

Wanting to win is not enough. You have to prepare to win. Winners do whatever it takes to get to the next level. Are you willing to do whatever it takes? If you're not, then your dream is a pipe-dream.

Put It Into Action:

Proper preparation prevents poor performance. Your coach or mentor will save you precious time by helping you focus on your strengths as you create your perfect plan.

Expect the best, plan for the worst and prepare to be surprised.

— Denis Waitley

"Leadership is influence. It's the ability to obtain followers. The key to success in any endeavor is the ability to lead others successfully."

— John Maxwell

PART IV
HOW TO BECOME
A BETTER LEADER

Walking the track in Sarajevo to learn the fastest lines that will result in the fastest times. Leaders are willing to do whatever it takes to improve their results.

**"Birds of a feather flock together.
Make sure you're in the right flock."**

— Ruben Gonzalez

Birds of a Feather

Who you surround yourself with will determine how far you go.

After I decided to take up the sport of luge and train for the 1988 Calgary Winter Olympics, decision making became pretty simple for me. I knew that every action I took in the next four years was either going to get me closer to my goal or pull me away from my goal. Everything I did would make a difference—even the people I associated with.

You see, there are two kinds of people in the world. They are either on your team or they are not on your team. They are either on your dream team or they are not. People will either encourage you or cast doubt. If they doubt you can do it, they could steal your dream away!

Associating with negative people makes us think negatively. Close contact with petty individuals develops petty habits in us. On the other hand, companionship with people who have big ideas raises the level of our thinking; close contact with ambitious people helps make us more ambitious.

I came to the realization that if someone laughed at my dream, they were laughing at me. If they did not believe in me, I stopped associating with them. I had to. They had the power to make me doubt myself and cause me to ultimately quit.

I was taking up the luge at the age of 21 - way too old! And I was trying to qualify for the Olympics just four years away! I could not leave anything to chance. I didn't have time to waste. I needed to know right away who was for me and who was not.

How did I do it? I told everyone I spoke with about my dream. If they laughed at me, rolled their eyes, or in any way showed lack of belief, I stopped associating with them. I could not afford to. They were a dream stealer. However, if they got excited about my dream, I held on to them like they were made of Gold! I'd just found myself a cheerleader – an encourager.

By doing this all the time, before long I could have filled a cheering section with my supporters. An unexpected benefit of doing this was that I created a positive pressure that kept me from quitting when the going got tough. You see, no matter how rough a day I was having at the track, it was going to be easier to get back on the sled than to come back home and tell everyone that I had quit.

Birds of a feather flock together. Make sure you're in the right flock. It's your choice.

Put It Into Action:

If you fly with eagles, you will think, feel and act like an eagle. Who are you spending most of your time with? Are you spending your time with the people who will lead you to your dream? Are you associating with people who encourage you and push you to take greater risks? Or, are you hanging around with people who are keeping you where you are? Ninety percent of success is a result of who you regularly associate with.

The Power of a Coach

Have you ever had someone tell you that you were destined to do great things in life? Did you buy into their belief in you? Sometimes, we have to rely on someone else's belief until our own belief kicks in.

When Bob Mathias was young, he was an anemic, sickly kid. His love for sports drove him to get involved in track and field in high school. Over time, Bob developed into a solid all-around athlete, but he was not national level in any one event.

Four months before the 1948 Olympic Games, his track coach, Virgil Thomas, believed in Bob so much that he told him, "Bob, you have four years. If you got started right away, you could possibly make the 1952 Olympics in the decathlon."

Coach Thomas' belief in Mathias was incredible because Mathias had never run the 1,500 meters, he had never pole-vaulted, he'd never thrown a javelin, and he had never even heard of the decathlon. To top it off, Mathias was only 17 years old!

However, Coach Thomas belief was so strong that Mathias

bought into it and started training right away. One month after he started training, Mathias competed in his first decathlon. Incredibly, he won first place! Two weeks later, he entered the U.S. Decathlon National Championship. He won again! Six weeks later, he was competing in the 1948 Summer Olympic Games. He had beaten his coach's prediction by four years!

Now Mathias was competing against athletes much older and much more experienced than he. They were the best athletes in the world. Incredibly, Mathias was not intimidated. He amazed the sports world at the age of 17 by becoming the youngest Decathlon Olympic Champion!

"**A coach or mentor will accelerate your success.**"

Mathias went on to win his second Olympic Decathlon in 1952. None of this would have been possible if his coach, his mentor, had not seen his greatness, believed in him, and encouraged him to pursue his dream.

When somebody compliments you, they've just seen a glimpse of your greatness. They have seen something about you that sticks out like a sore thumb—but it's so natural to you that you tend to discount it.

The next time someone compliments you, thank them and start using your God-given gifts to reach your dream. Surround yourself with winners, find a coach or mentor who believes in you, and win the Olympic Gold in your personal and professional life!

Put It Into Action:

Find a coach who believes in you and accelerate your success. Use your natural gifts to reach your dream. Put a lot of stock in other people's sincere compliments.

Leadership and Chick-fil-A

My first job in high school back in 1978 was working at Chick-fil-A. We had a horrible location in a dark corner on the second floor of a small shopping mall in Houston. Back then, Chick-fil-A had only 141 stores nationwide. But we were consistently in the top ten stores in sales.

Why did our store perform so well? It was all because of our manager's leadership. Our manager, Steve Mason, was a gung ho, motivator type who made working at a fast food restaurant a blast. Steve was always focused on making work fun and getting us to constantly produce at a high level. There was always some kind of a contest going on.

One time, he divided the crew into two teams and for a month ran an upselling contest... you know, "Would you like fries with that, sir?" Then he took the winning team to a five-star restaurant for a five-course brunch! After the contest, we had become so used to upselling our customers, we kept on doing it!

Steve constantly tied the store's goals to our personal goals, so we understood that we were employed by Chick-fil-A, but we were really working for ourselves. He helped us understand that the work ethic and the life skills we were learning would make us more successful in the future. Out of our crew came an Air Force officer, a college professor, an automotive service manager, an author and an Olympian…

Steve set high standards which attracted high achievers. Our crew stuck together and became tight. We worked for Steve for three years, and we still keep in touch 25 years later! This was unheard of in the fast food industry.

It didn't take long for the Chick-fil-A corporation to figure out that Steve was too valuable to just be running a store. Steve earned a well-deserved promotion. Today, Steve's in charge of Operations Services for Chick-fil-A.

Unfortunately, the manager who replaced Steve was not the leader Steve was, and within six months, we all quit. The restaurant ended up shutting down a few years after that.

Steve taught me a lot about leadership. He showed me that no matter what your circumstances are (in our case, a bad restaurant location), a leader can single-handedly create a winning environment, a winning culture, wherever they are. Leadership flows from the top down. It's not the other way around.

Start becoming the best leader you can be… at home, at work, at the little league field, and in your community. Become a better leader, and you'll attract top people to your team. As you do, you'll be changing the world around you!

Put It Into Action:

Associate with winners and top performers. Become the best leader you can be so you can attract and keep the best talent.

How to Become
a Better Leader

When I decided to take up the luge and train for the Olympics, I was 21 years old. Back then, I thought I could make it to the Olympics all by myself. I still had a lot of growing up to do...

In "Seven Habits of Highly Effective People," Steven Covey talks about three stages people go through—dependence, independence, and interdependence. At 21, I was still in the independent stage and needed to move on to becoming interdependent.

Along the way, I realized that I needed some help. In order to accomplish great things, I was going to have to develop some leadership and people skills to build a team. Then I would have to work through the team to make my Olympic dream come true. I was going to have to turn singles luge into a team sport. It's no different in any big project or endeavor. Lone rangers never accomplish as much as people who work through teams.

It takes two things to be a good leader—passion and integrity.

If you are passionate about your mission, you will attract people who are like minded, people who would like to be a part of your mission. I was passionate. I told everyone I talked to about my Olympic dream. Everyone! And, I was excited about it. I was not wishy-washy. Other people had no doubt that I believed in and was committed to the dream. By doing that, whenever I talked to someone who was interested in the Olympics, I became their link to the Olympic Games. Many times, they were willing to help me out.

Everyone has the capacity to be passionate about something. Unfortunately, most people keep their passion all bottled in. They don't want to show their passion out of fear of what others might think. I didn't care what others thought. I actually wanted to know who did not believe in me so I could stop associating with them.

The first part of leadership is passion for the cause. The second part is integrity.

Would you follow someone you don't trust? Of course not! So, if you want to be the leader and have others follow you, you need to be absolutely trustworthy. Your word is gold. You keep your word. You start being very careful about what you promise. You must deliver on every promise. Every time you don't, your credibility and your reputation suffer. The only way to become trustworthy in other people's eyes is to always under promise and over deliver. If you always do that, people will automatically trust you.

If you have passion for the cause and are a person of integrity, you'll be ahead of 95% of the people out there. People will be attracted to you, and you will be able to accomplish great things.

Put It Into Action:

How passionate are you about your dream? When people think about you, do they associate you with your dream? Make it a habit to under promise and over deliver. Always go the extra mile.

What Do You Stand For?

The top achievers in every field, the leaders, know who they are, what they believe in, and what they stand for. Knowing what they stand for keeps them from wasting precious time and energy, thus allowing them to accomplish many times more that the average person who has no clear goals or values.

You have to know what your values are because your values determine your beliefs. Your beliefs, in turn, determine your expectations. And your expectations determine your overall attitude and what you are willing to do to get the job done.

Bottom line, your actions will determine your results, but as you can see, your values and beliefs determine what actions you'll take. People are happiest when they act in ways that are in sync with their values. If you are acting against your values, you will not be happy. So, it is important to spend some time figuring out what your values are - because they will help you find the way to happiness.

One way of ensuring yourself that you are acting in harmony

with your values is to trust your intuition. Listen to and trust your gut feelings. Listen to your heart.

Some questions which will help you determine your main values are: What makes you feel good about yourself? What makes you feel important? What fills you with pride? What would you like to be known for? How would you like to be remembered?

> **"Your values determine your destiny."**

Remember, you will become what you think about most of the time. Successful people constantly think about what they want to accomplish, about how they will accomplish it, and about being true to themselves as they accomplish it. Successful people know they must stay true to their values.

Put It Into Action:

Write down three to five of your most important values. What are you best known for? What kind of person would you like to be if you knew you could not fail? Are you practicing these values on a daily basis? Write your own obituary. What do you want your friends and family to say about you at your funeral? What's something new you could start doing today to be more in harmony with your values? Start doing it today and watch your self esteem soar.

Developing Your Vision to Succeed

People generally become what they think about all the time. That's why it's so important to manage your thoughts. Successful people think about the future most of the time. They think about where they are going and about what they can do to get there. Average people focus on the present, the past, and on their obstacles.

The number one predictor of success in life is based on how long term your thinking is. If you focus on what you want to happen in the long term, while making decisions in the present, you'll be very successful. The further you focus into the future, the better decisions you'll make today and the greater chance you have of realizing your dream.

The biggest single obstacle people face when setting long-term goals is their self-limiting beliefs. When you allow your self-limiting beliefs to take control, you set goals far below what you are capable of achieving.

I made that mistake. I never believed that I could win an Olympic medal; consequently, I only set a goal to compete in the Olympics. I made it three times. But, what if I had set a goal to win a medal? I might have become an Olympic medalist. At the least, I would have placed higher than I did. Don't make that mistake. Aim as high as possible.

Imagine what your life would be like in five years if it were perfect in every way. Focus on creating your ideal life and you will overcome your self-limiting beliefs. I constantly imagined what it would be like to walk into the Opening Ceremonies. By doing that, I overcame my self-limiting beliefs that I could not become an Olympian. If I had instead imagined what it would be like to be a medalist, I would have overcome those self-limiting beliefs.

See how this works? If you vividly imagine it enough, you start believing it's possible. Once you believe it's possible, you start acting like it's possible. If you act like its possible long enough and if you take enough action, before long, you make it a reality.

Imagine you had all the time, talent, abilities, and resources you needed to create your perfect life. Imagine that you could not fail. Now, what would your perfect life be like? Where would you be living? What would your career look like? What kind of relationship would you have with your loved ones? How would you look and feel if you were in perfect health? Don't settle for smaller dreams and goals. Go for the gold! Big dreams have the power to inspire you to action and the power to inspire others to help you.

Now ask yourself, "How will I do this? What additional skills do I need to pull it off? What do I need to do every day to acquire those skills and become an expert in my field in five years? How will I do it?" If you keep asking yourself those key questions, the answers will come.

Once you start focusing and thinking about the future, start asking yourself how will you do it, and begin to take massive action, you will be a lot happier. That's because happiness is a byproduct of working hard to reach your goals and dreams.

Put It Into Action:

Focus on your long-term goals. Ask yourself "How will I do it?" When the answers come, take massive action in the pursuit of your goals and dreams.

Walking Your Talk

Leaders in every field agree that there is a shortage of people who get things done, of people who get results. That is great news. It's an opportunity for all of us. What that means is that if you want to move up in your field, all you have to do is to start getting results. So, how do you do that? By becoming a person of action—Massive Action!

Having good ideas is not enough. Even having great ideas is not enough. Ideas are a dime a dozen. However, people who implement ideas are priceless. Everything that exists in this world is the product of an idea that was acted upon, even the chair you're sitting in!

Successful people are active. They get things done. They don't waste any time. Successful people have an air of urgency about them. Passive people are not successful. Passive people procrastinate. They put things off. They wait for everything to be perfect before taking action.

Well, I've got news for you. Conditions have never been or

never will be perfect. What if Eisenhower had waited until conditions were perfect to invade Normandy? What if Kennedy had waited until conditions were perfect before deciding to put a man on the moon? What if Columbus had waited for conditions to be perfect before setting out on his voyage?

When you take a family vacation, you probably don't wait until all the lights are green. You get started, and you handle the red lights as you come across them. Use that approach with everything else.

Do something. Get started. Move! Get some momentum going. If you don't, you'll regret it and you will be filled with stress. Stress comes from not doing what you know you should be doing.

Once you get started, once you're in motion, your mind begins to focus on how to get the job done. As soon as you get in motion, you move ahead of the competition – all those poor souls that are still "thinking about it."

Action produces confidence. Inaction strengthens fear. Just think about when you were a kid on the high dive in your neighborhood pool. The longer you waited to dive, the worse the fear got. But once you decided to dive, the fear was gone and you spent the rest of the afternoon diving. Taking action made it fun. It made it exhilarating.

You know what you need to do. Do it now. Get going. Get started. Become an action fanatic! You'll be glad you did. If you're not willing to take action, do us all a favor and **STOP TALKING ABOUT IT!**

Put It Into Action:

What's the one thing you can do in the next 15 minutes that will propel your dream forward? Why aren't you doing it? Your new mantra needs to be "Do It Now!" "Do It Now!" "Do It Now!"

> **If your actions inspire others to dream more, learn more, do more and become more, you are a leader.**

— John Quincy Adams

"Desire is the key to motivation, but its determination and commitment to an unrelenting pursuit of your goal, that will enable you to attain the success you seek."

— Mario Andretti

PART V
COMMITTING
TO YOUR DREAM

Training in an ice rink in Houston.
Do the best you can with the resources you have.

**"Destiny is not a matter of chance.
It is a matter of choice.
It's not a thing to be waited for.
It is a thing to be achieved."**

— William Jennings Bryan

The Power to Choose

In his book "Roots," Alex Haley tells about something unexpected that happened right after slavery was abolished. The newly freed slaves did not know how to be free. All their lives, other people had made their decisions for them; consequently, they had never learned how to make choices. You could say their "choice-making muscles" needed developing. Many of the slaves actually stayed with their masters and worked for them for the rest of their lives.

In the movie "The Shawshank Redemption," when Brooks, the prison librarian who had been an inmate for 50 years, was set free, he didn't know how to be a free man. He didn't know how to use his power to choose. He had been told what to do all of his life. For Brooks, life as a free man was so overwhelming that he ended up committing suicide.

Most people's "choice-making muscles" could use a little strengthening. After all, when we are young, our parents and our teachers tell us what to do. Then, we get a job and our boss tells us what to do. It seems like there's always someone out there eager to tell us what to do – if we let them.

As a result, we start drifting through life, instead of designing our future. We start existing instead of living, and we end up using a fraction of our God-given gifts. We forget that we have the power to choose who we want to be, what we want to accomplish, where we want to live, etc. We stop taking responsibility for our results, and start living as a victim, instead of as a victor.

You and I have the power to choose what we do with our lives. You are where you are because of the choices you've made. If you don't like where you are, you need to start making different choices. It's not rocket science.

My Dad always told me, "It's not what happens to you, it's how you handle it!" He also said, "You have the power to choose your destiny." It wasn't until I started acting like I believed those things that my life started to become interesting.

I have a little secret for you. There is a magical moment between your circumstances and your results. That moment is called **choice**. When something happens to you, when circumstances happen to you, when things that seem unfair happen to you, don't whine and complain. The instant you start blaming your circumstances is the instant you become a victim. Once you do that, you can kiss your future goodbye. Remember, you can choose your response to those circumstances. Make a wise **choice**, handle it properly, and watch your results improve tremendously. What kind of life do you want? The good news is that you have the power to create it.

Once you stop making excuses and start taking responsibility for your results, your life will start to become really exciting. It did for me.

Put It Into Action:

Have you been making excuses? Don't you realize that **everyone** has challenges? Stop making excuses. Resolve to do something right now about what's holding you back. Resolve to become an inspiration to others who share your challenges.

You're Only Six Inches Away!

Back when I took up the sport of luge, one of my Olympic coaches used to tell me, "Ruben, you're only six inches away from massive success!" I wasn't sure what he meant. He explained, "Six inches is the distance between your ears. Your success depends on what you feed your mind." He was talking about the "Inner Game." It would be years before I really understood what he meant. Today, I realize that he was 100% right.

You always hear about the mental part of sports being more important than the physical part. I have to admit that I was always a bit skeptical. I was skeptical until a cold morning in October, 1998.

I took up the sport of luge in 1984, and I retired from the luge right after the 1992 Albertville Olympics. After Albertville, I didn't take a luge run for six years. However, during those six years, I read hundreds of books on success and listened to thousands of motivational tapes. I didn't realize it, but by doing that, I was becoming mentally tougher.

In 1998, six years after retiring from the luge, I decided to begin training for the 2002 Salt Lake City Olympics. My first day of training was unforgettable. I was at the start of the Calgary luge track, ready to take my first run in six years. Surprisingly, I was feeling cool, calm, and confident. Believe it or not, my first four runs were personal bests! I felt like I had more control of the sled than ever before. Four personal bests after a six year break! Unbelievable! On that day, I stopped being a skeptic. That day, I became a believer in the power of the human mind.

Olympic athletes use many mental training techniques to sharpen their competitive edge—techniques designed to keep them hungry, confident, and mentally tough so they'll do what it takes to win. These are techniques anyone can use to get better results in their personal or professional life.

Olympic athletes use subliminal techniques to help them reach their goals. The walls of my office are covered with Olympic memorabilia. I surround myself with pictures which constantly bombard my mind with where I want to go. Doing this helps me become unstoppable on the way to my goals.

I even use vision board software in my computer that helps me stay focused on my goals. My favorite feature is that it allows me to write my own affirmations and post pictures of my own goals. The software lets you customize it specifically for your own goals—becoming a better salesperson, becoming a better student, improving your golf game, and so on. It puts you in the driver's seat.

This software is not magic. It's simply a tool you can use to help you do what you know you need to do to succeed. I wish this had been available years ago. Because success doesn't just happen. Success requires massive action. Thomas Edison said, "Genius is 2% inspiration and 98% perspiration." The key to success in anything is getting ourselves to take consistent and persistent action. (You can learn more about this goal achievement tool by visiting my website.)

What do you want to accomplish? Better sales? A promotion at work? Better grades? How bad do you want it? Do you want it bad enough to get the tools that will help program yourself to take action? Remember, you're only six inches away!

Put It Into Action:

Surround yourself with pictures of your goals and dreams. Be willing to use any tool or technique that will increase your odds of realizing your goals.

The Right Way
to Use Affirmations

When Muhammad Ali said, "I am the Greatest!" He was doing several things at once; he was psyching out his opponents, he was branding himself, he was getting publicity, but most importantly, he was conditioning his subconscious mind to help him *become* "The Greatest."

You can program your subconscious mind to become an automatic "guiding system" that will help you realize your goals, dreams, and aspirations.

Affirmations, also known as "self-talk" are precise statements that describe goals in their completed state, such as "I am enjoying the benefits of living in my dream home in the Rocky Mountains," or "I am feeling light, trim, and fit in my ideal body weight of 185 lbs."

In order for affirmations to effectively be picked up by your subconscious mind, they must have certain characteristics; they must start with the words "I am," they must be written in the present tense, and they must be stated in the positive, not in the negative.

The subconscious mind does not understand negatives. It understands word pictures. So, if you said, "I never overeat," it would understand, "I overeat." Affirmations must be short and sweet. They must be precise, not general. "I'm fit and trim," is not as powerful as "I'm a fit and trim 175 lbs."

The best time to read your affirmations is first thing in the morning or last thing at night. Read them with passion and emotion, preferably while looking at yourself in the mirror.

One of the most powerful affirmations you can use is "The Champion's Creed." I've used it for years.

To get your own free copy, visit TheChampionsCreed.com.

Reading affirmations will put you in a strong, determined state of mind. Determination is a powerful state of mind because when you are determined to do something, nothing will make you quit.

> **Condition your mind to succeed.**

Read your affirmations with power and energy whenever you need to do something challenging, like making a presentation, making an important sales call, or whenever you need an edge to be your best.

Put It Into Action:

Read your affirmations with power, passion, and energy.

Starting Your Day Like a Champion

The quality of your state of mind determines the quality of your results in whatever you do. The things you do first thing in the morning set your mental tone for the rest of the day. I challenge you to get radical for the next 30 days and do something you have never done before.

If you do this for the next 30 days, you will dramatically change your attitude, your focus, your intensity, and will be a different person. Your friends and family will ask, "What happened to you?" Trust me—if you do this for 30 days, you'll want to do it for the rest of your life.

For the next 30 days:

1. Go to bed 30 minutes earlier - no more late night TV. You'll need to get up early tomorrow.

2. When you go to bed, think about how it will feel when you realize your dream.

3. Get up 30 minutes earlier. Don't turn on your computer.

These first 30 minutes will set the tone for the rest of your day and the rest of your life.

4. Take a minute to write down your goals and dreams. You must write your goals down every day. Writing your goals down is an act of commitment that focuses your mind to take action (and to be successful, action is the name of the game).

5. Take three minutes to write down **why** you want those dreams. What's driving you? Be specific. If your **why** is big enough the How will take care of itself.

6. Stand in front of a mirror and read your Champion's Creed Card. Read it with power and passion, like you mean it. Get your Champion's Creed card here: www. TheChampionsCreed.com.

7. Close your eyes and vividly imagine what it will feel like when you actually make your dream a reality. Get all your senses involved and allow yourself to get passionate.

8. Write down the three most important things you must do today to get you closer to your dream—then, do them sometime today! Many people get great results by doing this step the night before.

9. Read for 15 to 20 minutes from a positive, inspiring, motivating book.

10. On the way to work, rather than listening to the radio, listen to a positive, inspiring, motivating self-development CD (Zig Ziglar, Les Brown, Denis Waitley, Brian Tracy).

I guarantee that if you do this for the next 30 days, your life WILL change, because your attitude will change.

Going from Wishful Thinking to Commitment

When I became fascinated with the idea of becoming an Olympian, I was able to hold on to that vision, even though it would involve many years of training. People tell me I must have a lot of willpower. I don't think I have any more than most people. What I had was an enormous fascination with the thought of becoming an Olympian, and I had the desire to make it happen. It was the fascination with the end result that kept me going.

Dreams are very fragile things. Whenever you have a dream, you must nurture and protect it so it will gain strength and so you'll have time to develop the belief that it is possible.

If you don't nurture your dream, it will simply remain a fantasy. Fantasies do not come to fruition, because when your dream is a fantasy, you are operating out of wishful thinking. Wishful thinking is when you are not doing anything and hoping your dream will somehow fall on your lap.

Sooner or later, you have to become committed to your dream and start taking action. Commitment comes when you stop listening to your fears and start listening to your inner voice. That is the voice that urges you to pursue your dream.

When you stop taking council from your fears and start taking council from your heart, your dream will gain strength and you'll become a person on a mission, a person who will not be satisfied until they reach their dream. Success is a decision. It's an inside job. You just have to believe.

You must hold onto your dream and know it like you know your name. Can you imagine someone trying to convince you that your name was not really your name? You'd look at them like they were crazy. You'd think to yourself, "This person has no clue!"

Well, that's exactly how you need to react when someone questions your capacity to achieve your dream. Whenever someone laughs at your dream, you've just run into someone who does not believe as much as you do. Stop associating with anyone like that. Don't waste your time trying to convince them. You'll be wasting precious time and energy you could be using to reach your dream. Just smile, run, and think, "Just watch me, Buster!"

If someone asks you what makes you think you can achieve that, simply say, "I just know because I know." Don't allow others to let you settle for anything less than your dreams. You have a champion inside who is urging you to pursue your dream. Listen to your heart and go for it! Accept the challenge so you can experience the exhilaration of victory.

Put It Into Action:

Protect your dream and nurture your dream. Don't waste your time with people who don't believe in you. Associate only with people who believe and encourage you.

Decide You Will
Get the Last Laugh

The four world-class sprinters had a dream to compete in the summer Olympics in track and field. When they failed to qualify, rather than having a pity party, they put their heads together to think of another way to make their Olympic Dream a reality. After brainstorming for solutions, they decided to become bobsledders and go for the Winter Olympics.

It would be the first time a bobsled team from Jamaica would compete in the Olympics. Jamaican bobsled? "Inconceivable!" said most people. But they were great athletes—extremely fast. They just needed to master their new sport's techniques. The fact they came from Jamaica was completely immaterial. The only fact that mattered was whether they were willing to put themselves through the struggle.

I chatted with them briefly at the 1988, 1992, and 2002 Olympics. When they were just getting started at the '88 Calgary Olympics, everyone laughed at them – sometimes to their face. They were experiencing what pioneers in every field experience – lots of ridicule.

When I asked them how everyone's mockery made them feel, they replied, "Just watch us. We're not quitters. We'll get the last laugh."

A few days later, during the '88 Olympic competition, they had a horrific crash (you've probably seen it in their movie, "Cool Runnings"). When you watch the crash, as the bobsled flips and smashes into the wall, it looks like the driver's neck is snapping. Incredibly, Stokes, the driver, walked away from the crash. Stokes walked away from the crash, but not away from bobsledding. The Jamaicans refused to quit. They **were** going to have the last laugh.

Four years later at the Albertville Olympics, a few people were still laughing, but no longer to their faces. The Jamaicans were gaining experience. By the 2002 Salt Lake City Olympics, their fifth Olympics, the Jamaicans were beating some solid teams. No one was laughing now – except the Jamaicans! By now, they had earned the admiration of people from all over the world.

What I learned from the Jamaican Bobsledders is that no matter who you are, whenever you try something new, something different, something daring and bold, people always react in the same way. At first, they laugh at you, then, they watch you to see if you quit or not, and finally, if you persist, they admire you. But, it's up to you to endure while everyone else is laughing.

That's why it's so important to build a Dream Team of supporters—a group of people who believe in you and encourage you through the tough times.

The next time you're doing something bold and courageous and people are laughing at you, do what the Jamaicans did. DECIDE you will get the last laugh.

Put It Into Action:

Create a Dream Team of believers who will help you persist through other peoples' laughter and disbelief. Decide to get the last laugh. It's your choice!

Commit to Excellence

Most successful people have something very important in common. Somewhere along the line, they made a decision to commit to becoming the best they could be in their field. They committed to excellence.

They realized that if they became the best in their field, the rewards would more than make up for the effort. So, they made a decision to pay the price, do whatever they could, and make any sacrifice to become an expert in their field.

Once they acquired the skills and knowledge, which anyone can do, they started earning many times what the average people in their field were earning. No matter where you are today, you can make a decision to commit to becoming the best. You can do it. Everyone who is now an expert in their field was once only getting started. They just made a decision, learned the skills, and started taking action.

It won't be easy, but it's doable. It's possible, and the rewards make it more than worthwhile. You can change. You can improve. You can be better. You can do more. We all can. You can learn the skills that will propel you to the next level. It's just a decision away.

Once you make the decision to increase your skills and knowledge on the road to becoming an expert in your field, you'll quickly move ahead of the pack. It will feel like you're running a race without competition because hardly anyone else even thinks of making that kind of commitment.

> **"Become an expert in your field."**

Ask yourself: What knowledge and skills do I need to master to become the best in my field? What would I have to know? If you don't know, go to the experts in your field and ask **them**. They will help you if they see that you are committed to excellence.

I'm constantly meeting with the experts in my field to learn what I need to do to win more. I rely on my coaches to help me do the right things and to keep me from doing the things that will keep me from achieving my goals.

If you find an arena that you are suited to play in, commit to excellence, and apply what your coaches and mentors teach you, people will be amazed at how much you accomplish in your lifetime.

Put It Into Action:

Regularly meet with experts in your field to learn what you need to do to win more. Become a lifelong learner. Find a coach or mentor who can take your game to the next level.

The Power of Being Flexible

We live in times of constant and rapid change. Because of this, one of the most important qualities you can develop to succeed in the 21st century is flexibility. Flexibility means approaching life's circumstances with an open mind, ever ready to make course changes.

The opposite of flexibility is rigidity and hard-headedness - the unwillingness to change in the face of new circumstances. You must learn to be flexible because whenever circumstances change, the person who adapts first will win.

Some people focus on how things "should" be. Things will seldom be as they should be, so focusing on what should be is a waste of time and energy. "Should be's" are meaningless. The only thing that matters is what is.

Whenever you are trying to accomplish something, don't worry too much about how you "should" go about getting results. Focus on whether you **are** getting results. Is your approach working? If not, change your approach.

Be open to new ideas and information. One new idea could literally transform your life. It could make you a fortune or cause you to lose a fortune. That is why reading is so critical to success. In the information age, whoever has the best information **and acts on it**, wins. That's why having a coach or mentor is so important. Coaches are experts in their field; they are counselors who provide the **best** information.

There are three statements that you need to use if you want to be more flexible. These statements are tough to use, but they will save you time, energy, grief, and pain. The first one is, "I was wrong." The second one is, "I made a mistake." And the third one is, "I changed my mind."

" Set a goal. Plan. Execute. " Adjust as you go.

Start using these phrases and you'll instantly become more productive. The next time you realize you were wrong, you made a mistake, or you changed your mind about something, say so, and everybody will get on with resolving the problem or achieving the goal.

Admitting you were wrong, you made a mistake, or you changed your mind is not being weak. On the contrary - it's a mark of courage and character. People will look up to you.

It's tough to use these phrases; but if you want to accomplish great things, you need to make a decision to put your ego aside. You see, you can either be right or you can be rich. It's your choice.

Put It Into Action:

Always focus on results. Be open to trying new approaches to reaching your goals.

How to Hit Your Goals in Half the Time

Would you like to be able to reach your goals in half the time? Would you like to have a greater sense of control over your life?

People who have a sense of control over their lives are happier and more confident than people who feel out of control. A big part of achieving that sense of control is learning how to manage your time.

Once you have a clear goal you are working toward, you must decide two things. Number one, decide to start doing the things that will bring you closer to your goal and stop doing the things that will keep you from your goal, and two, decide to work on the most important tasks first.

In actuality, you will not be managing time. You will be managing yourself so you can take maximum advantage of your time. That's because you really can't manage time. Time keeps on moving forward and there's nothing we can do about it. What you will be doing is setting priorities and focusing on your priorities.

The first step in time management is to make a list of the tasks you'll need to complete in order to achieve each of your goals and to prioritize your list. The second step in managing your time is to start planning your weeks and your days in advance. Sunday evening is a great time to plan your week, and the end of your workday is a great time to plan your next day. Remember…plans change, but the act of planning gets you to think about the road ahead and saves you time in the long run.

Why plan the night before? Because if you do, your subconscious mind will work on your task list all night long. Often, you'll wake up in the morning with ideas and insights that will help you during the day.

Prioritizing your tasks is critical because whenever you work on a particular task, you are choosing not to work on all of the other tasks. The choice you make of which tasks to work on will determine your future. Do you want to leave your future to chance, or is your future worth planning for?

Once you start working on a task, work on it until it is completed. Focus on only one task at a time. Thomas Edison said that his success was due to his ability to work continuously on one task until he was finished. If it's good enough for Edison, don't you think its good enough for you and me?

Plan your day in such a way that it will give you long, uninterrupted chunks of work time—60 to 90 minute chunks of time. When your mind is focused on a single task for long periods of time, you will accomplish many times more work than if you are working on several tasks simultaneously.

Finally, learn to say "No" to anything that will keep you from achieving your goals. Focus single-mindedly on your desired end result, and you will be amazed at how much you achieve in your life.

Put It Into Action:

Plan ahead. Prioritize your tasks. Work only on important tasks. Focus on one task at a time. Stick to your plan.

> " **The quality of a person's life is in direct proportion to their commitment to excellence.** "
>
> — Vince Lombardi

"Expect trouble as an inevitable part of life, and when it comes, hold your head high, look it squarely in the eye and say, 'I will be bigger than you. You cannot defeat me.'

— Ann Landers

PART VI
OVERCOMING CHALLENGES ON THE WAY TO THE TOP

A bad day at the track. Broken foot, broken hand, totaled sled, and an early end to a luge season.

"The number of times you succeed is in direct proportion to the number of times you fail and keep trying.

— Tom Hopkins

The Price of Success

Average people expect their dreams and goals to fall on their lap. They're not willing to inconvenience themselves for their dreams. They refuse to do anything outside their comfort zone to reach their dreams. They don't stand for anything, they don't commit to anything, and they drift through life. That's why they are average—because they are not willing to do what successful people are willing to do. Consequently, they don't live life; they merely exist. They just take up space.

In order to succeed in life, you have to be willing to inconvenience yourself in a big way. You have to be willing to commit to yourself and your dream. You have to be willing to face your fears and do some things that are very uncomfortable. You have to be willing to do the things average people are not willing to do. You see, success is not about aptitude. It's about attitude. It's about having the attitude that you are willing to do whatever it takes to get the job done.

General William Westmoreland once reviewed a platoon of paratroopers in Vietnam. As he went down the line, he asked each of them a question: "How do you like jumping, son?" "Love it, sir!" was the first answer. "How do you like jumping?" he asked the next. "The greatest experience in my life, sir!" exclaimed the paratrooper. "How do you like jumping?" he asked the third. "I hate it, sir," he replied. "Then why do you do it?" asked Westmoreland. "Because I want to be around guys who love to jump." Yeah! That guy had the right attitude!

One day, I was talking with Rudy Ruettiger, the inspiration behind the movie, "Rudy," and I mentioned that I didn't like the luge. I told Rudy that I competed in the luge because it was my vehicle to the Olympics. Rudy got a kick out of that. Then, he told me; "I never liked football. My dream was to be part of the Notre Dame Tradition, and I saw football as a way to do **that!**"

Sometimes, you have to do things you don't like to do in order to get where you want to go. The paratrooper was willing to jump out of airplanes so he could hang around people who loved to jump. I was willing to hurl myself down the ice in order to compete in the Olympics. Rudy was willing to get beat up on the football field in order to get to be a part of the Notre Dame tradition.

How about you? Is there something that's been holding you back from your dream? Has something been keeping you from taking action? Don't let anything keep you from your dream. I guarantee that the feeling you experience once you realize your dreams and aspirations will make the price you paid feel worthwhile.

The price of success is big, but the price of regret that comes from not pursuing your dream is a hundred times bigger. Make a decision that you will do whatever it takes to realize your goals and dreams and make your life an adventure.

Put It Into Action:

Act in spite of your fear. Be willing to inconvenience yourself as you pursue your dreams.

Eliminating Your Obstacles

Success is about getting from point A to point B. It's about knowing where you are and knowing where you want to end up. Success simply means you set a goal and you reached it.

Success is simple, but not easy. Most people allow fear of failure to keep them from even attempting to pursue their dreams. They don't understand that failure is part of the price of success. You need to expect to fail and fall short many times before you reach your goals. That's just how life is. Since you will have many failures on the road to success, it is very important to learn how to remove the obstacles, roadblocks, and bottlenecks that are between you and your goals.

Once you've decided upon a goal, write down all the obstacles that you think might be slowing you down. Now, focus on finding solutions to your obstacles. This might sound simplistic, but the fact is that if you focus all your energy into attacking your obstacles, you **will** eliminate them and accelerate your progress.

Einstein said that you cannot solve your problems with the same level of thinking that created them, so you will need help. This is where having a mentor or a coach can help you win even more.

Successful people don't quit. They simply focus on finding solutions to their problems. If you want the outcome bad enough, you'll figure out a way. And every time you find the solution to a problem, your 'solution-finding' muscles get stronger. Solution finding is a skill that will improve with use.

There are bottlenecks on the way to every goal. Your ability to look ahead and remove bottlenecks will help you reach your goals faster than you can imagine. You can anticipate bottlenecks either through your experience, or through the experience of your mentors and coaches.

Typically, 80% of the bottlenecks will be within you. You are the biggest barrier to reaching your dreams. Successful people understand this. That is why they invest so much time in self-development. Successful people understand that the better they become, the better their results will be.

Fear and doubt are the two things that keep most people from having the courage to succeed. Most people simply don't believe in themselves. That is why the books you read and the people you associate with can have such a huge impact in your life. One way to overcome fear and doubt is by acquiring knowledge and skills. If you know how to do something, you become more confident. The knowledge comes from what you read and from who you associate with.

Once you determine what obstacle is holding you back, set a goal of overcoming that obstacle. By setting a goal to remove an obstacle, you are taking control of your life and your results and your confidence will improve. Don't just set a goal. Set a deadline, come up with a plan, and get to work. Once you remove the major obstacle that is holding you back, you will start making quantum leaps toward your goals and dreams.

Put It Into Action:

Identify bottlenecks that are keeping you from achieving your goals and tackle them one by one. Consult with your mentor.

Bouncing Back
Quickly to Win

Back in 1938, Karoly Takacs of the Hungarian Army was the top pistol shooter in the world. He was expected to win the gold in the 1940 Olympic Games scheduled to be held in Tokyo. Those expectations vanished one terrible day, just months before the Olympics. While training on military maneuvers with his squad, a hand grenade exploded in Takacs' right hand. Takacs' shooting hand was blown off.

Takacs spent a month in the hospital, depressed due to both the loss of his hand and the end to his Olympic dream. At that point, most people would have quit and would have probably spent the rest of their life feeling sorry for themselves. Takacs was a winner, though. Winners know that they can't let circumstances keep them down. They understand that life is hard and that they can't let life beat them down. Winners know in their heart that quitting is not an option.

Takacs picked himself up, dusted himself off, and decided to learn how to shoot with his left hand! His reasoning was simple.

He simply asked himself, "Why not?" Instead of focusing on what he didn't have – a world class right shooting hand, he decided to focus on what he did have – incredible mental toughness and a healthy left hand he could develop to shoot like a champion.

Takacs practiced by himself. No one knew what he was doing. Maybe he didn't want to subject himself to people who most certainly would have discouraged him from his rekindled dream. In the spring of 1939, he showed up at the Hungarian National Pistol Shooting Championship. Other shooters approached Takacs to give him their condolences and to congratulate him on having the strength to come watch them shoot. They were surprised when he said, "I didn't come to watch; I came to compete." They were even more surprised when Takacs won!

" **Trials teach us what we are made of.** "

In 1948, Takacs qualified for the London Olympics. At the age of 38, Takacs won the Gold Medal and set a new world record in rapid fire pistol shooting. Four years later, Takacs won the Gold Medal at the 1952 Helsinki Olympics. Takacs—a man with the mental toughness to bounce back from anything.

Winners in every field have a special trait that helps them become unstoppable. It's a special characteristic that allows them to survive major setbacks on the road to success. Winners recover **quickly**. Bouncing back is not enough. Winners bounce back **quickly**. They take their hit, they experience their setback, they have the wind taken out of their sails, but they **immediately** recover. Right away, they force themselves to look at the bright side of things – ANY bright side, and they say to themselves, "That's okay. There is always a way. I will find a way." They dust themselves off and pick up where they left off.

The reason quick recovery is important is that if you recover quickly, you don't lose your momentum and your drive. Takacs recovered in only one month. If he had wallowed in his misery, if he had played the martyr and felt sorry for himself much longer, he would have lost his mental edge – his "eye of the tiger" and he never would have been able to come back.

When a boxer gets knocked down, he has ten seconds to get back up. If he gets up in eleven seconds, he loses the fight. Remember that next time you get knocked down.

Takacs definitely had a right to feel sorry for himself. He had a right to stay depressed and to ask "Why me?" for the rest of his life. But Takacs made the decision to dig deep inside and find a solution, to pick himself up, and learn to shoot all over again. Winners always search for a solution. Losers always search for an escape.

The next time you get knocked down, act like a winner. Act like Takacs. Get up quickly, and astound the world!

Put It Into Action:

The next time life knocks you down, pretend you are a boxer that **must** do whatever it takes to get back up in 10 seconds…or else. Focus on how quickly you can get back up. Because the longer you're down, the harder it will be to regain your momentum. Remember, a setback is a setup for a comeback.

"The greatest glory in living lies not in never failing, but in rising every time we fail.

— Nelson Mandela

Even Cancer Could not Stop Her

A couple of days after finishing my competition at the Salt Lake City Olympics, I was sitting in the Olympic Village coffee shop drinking an espresso. There, I met an incredible lady, Ildiko Strehli of Hungary.

She was in her mid 30's and I was 39, so we both stood out like sore thumbs amongst the other athletes. (The average age for winter Olympians is early 20's. When you walk in the Olympic Village, it feels like you're on a college campus where everybody's in great shape. I looked so much older than the other athletes that almost every day someone would ask me if I was a coach!).

I asked her what her story was—how she'd gotten to the Olympics. Her story blew me away! Ever since she was eight years old, Ildiko Strehli had dreamed of competing in the Olympics in the bobsled. Well, she was about 25 years ahead of her time because women's bobsled did not become an Olympic sport until 2002.

Ildiko was a ski instructor in Park City when it was announced that there would be a Women's Bobsled competition in the Salt

Lake City Olympics. She had only four years to train and go for it. Right away, she signed up for bobsled driving school in Park City. But she couldn't do it alone. She had to create a Bobsled team from scratch. Ildiko went home to Hungary, held tryouts to look for a strong and fast teammate to be the "brakeman." The brakeman helps push the sled at the start and brakes the sled at the end of the run. A Hungarian discus thrower, Eva Kurti became her brakeman.

Now, they had a team but no sled. So, Ildiko maxed out her credit cards, bought a sled, and started training. Only the top 15 sleds in the world would get to compete in the Olympics. Two years before Salt Lake City, Ildiko was diagnosed with

"Find a higher purpose."

breast cancer and had to get a double mastectomy. As she was lying in the hospital, she thought, "It's all over. How can I train for the Olympics? I barely have enough strength to walk!"

When Ildiko was in the depths of her discouragement and depression, Eva brought Ildiko Lance Armstrong's book *"It's Not About the Bike: My Journey Back to Life."* The book is about how Armstrong had overcome cancer to win the Tour de France race over and over again. Ildiko got excited about the possibilities and was filled with a higher purpose. She decided, "I won't do this for myself. I'm going to qualify for the Olympics to show cancer survivors that they can realize their dreams, too."

She painted a pink ribbon with the words "Sled Full of Hope" on the side of their bobsled, and started training again. Against all odds, Ildiko and Eva qualified in the 15th spot and became Winter Olympians.

When Ildiko told me her story, I had tears in my eyes. I told her, "Ildiko, you are what the Olympics are all about. You truly have the Olympic spirit. I don't care whether you won a medal or not. I'd rather know you than all the other medal winners combined!

She smiled and said, "I just wanted cancer survivors to understand that cancer can change your life, but you can't let it change you. Don't be afraid to dream and to dream big. If I can do it, so can they."

No matter how bad your circumstances are, if you believe something is possible, and if you can find a higher purpose to inspire you to do the work, you can realize your dreams.

Put It Into Action:

Find a higher purpose that will inspire you to reach your dream. Surround yourself with people who will not let you quit. Find a coach or mentor who won't let you quit.

Notice the pattern yet? Successful people do anything that will increase their probability of success. They are willing to do whatever it takes to reach their goals. They stack the deck in their favor so that when life deals them a bad hand, they can recover and keep from quitting.

That's why having a coach or mentor is so critical. And that's why associating with like-minded people is so critical.

Go out and rent the movie "Miracle," about the US Hockey Team beating the Russians in the 1980 Lake Placid Olympics. They never would have done it without their coach.

While you're at it, watch "Rocky." Do you think that Rocky would have gone as far without his coach, Mick? Sure, Rocky is fictional, but have you ever seen any pro athlete that didn't have a coach?

Your life is a lot more important than a game or a sports championship. Don't you think you deserve to have someone in your corner, as well? Remember, the best way to cross a minefield is to follow somebody—preferably someone who has already crossed it!

"My strength lies solely in my tenacity."

— Louis Pasteur

How to Eliminate Your Self-Limiting Beliefs

The only way to improve your life is to change your beliefs about yourself and about your possibilities. Only when you believe something is possible, will you take action.

Would you like to double your income? Who wouldn't? But here's the rub—do you believe it's possible? If you don't, you will not do what you need to do to double it.

Who are you associating with? I make it a point to hang around people who are making many times what I'm making. I was on the phone with two millionaires just this morning. By doing that, you know what is happening? I'm starting to believe that I can do it, too. It's all about what you sincerely believe.

I guarantee that if I didn't make it a priority to regularly associate with millionaires, I would not believe that I can become a millionaire. By the way, these mentors of mine are doing the same thing, except they add a few zeroes. The millionaires are hanging around billionaires. No joke.

You see, it's no different than what you tell your kids. A C student can't teach you how to become a B student and a B student can't teach you how to become an A student. If all you do is hang around average people, I can tell you exactly what will happen. Before long, you'll start believing you have average intelligence, average creativity, average talent, average capability, and average skills. And you know what? In virtually every case, those beliefs will be **wrong**.

When you start associating with winners, you start realizing that they are not much smarter, talented, or gifted than most people. You start realizing that they are ordinary people with extraordinary desire, belief, focus, and willingness to get the job done. You hang around them long enough and you start seeing the possibilities. You start

Take control of your beliefs.

seeing that you've had what it takes all along. You start developing hope, belief, and faith in the future. When that starts happening, look out! You start taking action. Because when there's hope in the future, there's power in the present.

All beliefs are acquired. Beliefs are learned—and unlearned. You need to start believing that you have what it takes. Because you do. The next time you have a self-limiting belief, say to yourself, "What if that was not true at all?" Start thinking about yourself differently. Once you do, your life will change. You will start doubling and tripling your income. You'll learn new skills and take on new challenges. You will set bigger goals and start throwing your heart into achieving them. You'll start taking charge of your life.

You need to believe that you are destined to be a big success in life - whatever that means to you. Start saying it to yourself, "I am destined to be a big success in life." Once you believe it, you will act as if everything that happens to you is part of a great plan to make you successful. That's what happened to me, and it will happen to you, too.

Even when I broke bones on the luge, I believed that something good would come from it. I just believed it was part of the plan. I believed that anything that didn't kill me would make me stronger. You need to believe that way, too. Every time I had a setback, I looked for the lesson hidden within it. I set it up in my mind that, no matter what happened, I would win. That helped me from getting discouraged along the way. When you start thinking like that, nothing can stop you.

Make it a priority to manage your thoughts and people will be amazed at what you accomplish.

Put It Into Action:

Take control of your beliefs. You have greatness within you. Don't settle for second best. Become an inverse paranoid. A paranoid person believes that the world is conspiring to hurt them. An inverse paranoid believes that the whole world is conspiring to help them. Inverse paranoids understand that whenever one door closes, God will open a bigger, better door.

> **Even after a bad harvest there must be sowing.**
>
> — Seneca

What's Holding You Back?

Most people look at their obstacles and all they see is a reason why they can't make their dream a reality. They look at the obstacle, become discouraged (they lose heart), and they quit. Winners look at the obstacles, get mad, and then become determined to overcome them.

When I decided to take up the sport of luge and train for the Olympics four years away, I knew I had two major obstacles to overcome. Two things **had** to happen or else I would be watching the Olympics on TV: first, I had to learn how to luge (back then I couldn't even spell luge) and second, I had to be ranked in the top 50 lugers in the world to qualify to compete in the Olympics. I would only have two luge seasons to learn how to slide, because during the last two seasons, I needed to race internationally to work on my world ranking. Most people would have looked at those obstacles and quit before they got started!

You can read the story of how I did it and how I used the same principles to build several successful businesses in my book "*The*

Courage to Succeed." It's all about developing mental toughness. You can develop the mental toughness to look at an obstacle and become fired up and excited about the challenge ahead.

Often, all you have to do to overcome your roadblocks is to simply learn some new skills. Other times, you might have to refine some skills. You might have to enlist the help of other people. I did! Big time! You might have to create a team. Most of the time the roadblock is internal – lack of belief and doubt that you can pull it off.

> **Take a leap of faith. Jump and the net will appear.**

The roadblocks are not a bad thing. They are simply road signs that tell you what you need to work on next and where your focus needs to be. Your roadblocks help define what your goals need to be.

What's keeping you from realizing your dreams? What's the one thing that's slowing down all your progress? Your job is to identify the roadblocks and focus all your energy on doing whatever it takes to remove them. Once you do that, your dreams will be there for the taking.

Put It Into Action:

List the three main things that are keeping you from your dream. What can you do today to overcome those challenges? Who do you know that has had and has overcome those challenges? Call them up, take them out for coffee, and find out how they did it – they'll be glad to help. Successful people like to talk about their success. Have your coach or mentor help you come up with a plan to eliminate your roadblocks so you can develop momentum.

How to Turn
Defeat into Victory

I'll never forget it. We were training for a week in Sarajevo, Yugoslavia, an ancient city in Eastern Europe. We had a couple of hours to kill so we visited the old city. The streets in Old Sarajevo are too narrow for vehicles. The air is filled with smoke because many people still burn wood for heat. And everywhere you look you see towering minarets, a constant reminder that you are now in Eurasia, far from home. Walking the cobbled streets of Old Sarajevo makes you feels like you have been transported back in time.

Imagine my surprise when I walked into a smoke-filled café for a hot cup of Turkish coffee and heard the TV blaring in English! Back then, **nobody** spoke English in Sarajevo. Everyone spoke Serbo-Croatian. The TV was tuned in to ESPN! I was hooked! That cold morning, I saw a commercial I'll never forget. You've probably seen it, too. This is how the commercial went...

"Over 3,000 times I've been called upon by my company to perform, and I did not do what I was expected to do. Twenty-six times the company has called on me for the day's final activities, and I failed. Three hundred times I've been a part of my company's total failure. And I'm still considered to be the greatest basketball player that has ever lived. I'm Michael Jordan."

"Three thousand times I've been called upon to shoot the basketball at the basket and missed. Twenty-six times my team has asked me to shoot the final shot in the game, and I missed. I've been part of over 300 losses of the Chicago Bulls."

Act in spite of your fear.

"The next time the Bulls play and there are two to three seconds left in the game everyone knows who will be called to take the last shot. He is not afraid of losing. He is not afraid of defeat."

Wow! Michael Jordan's commercial came at a good time for me. At the time, the track in Sarajevo was the fastest in the world. We reached speeds of over 95 miles per hour from the Men's Start. At that speed, you feel like you're a cassette player stuck on fast forward and you can't find the stop button! I don't know about the other guys, but I felt fear on every run. I just got myself to act in spite of fear so I could make my dream come true.

And that's exactly what YOU need to do. *Act in spite of your fears.* Every time you do something you fear, you gain strength, confidence, courage, and faith. You must always stop and look fear in the face and do what you think you cannot do. How do you do that? Simple: by finding a dream big enough to overcome your fears, a dream that takes your breath away.

Any successful person will tell you the same thing. They'll tell you that they failed themselves to success. I have taken a couple of thousand luge runs since 1984. Out of all those runs, I remember only two runs that I was really proud of. Two luge runs that I nailed! I was proud of them, but even **that** is relative. I'll bet my coach, who was a three-time World Champion, thought that even those two runs were nothing to brag about! But you know what? Those two thousand "failures" got me to the Olympics three times. I failed my way to success. You could say I crashed my way to the top!

If your dream is big enough, you'll be able to go from one failure to another without losing enthusiasm. Before long, you'll look back and you'll see those failures for what they really were: success school. The failures you experience give you the education you need to begin to succeed. Once you start to succeed, the trick is to learn to go from one success to another without losing humility.

The Turkish coffee was a little strong, but I'm sure glad I walked into that Sarajevo coffee shop…

Put It Into Action:

Act in spite of your fears. If you do what you fear, the fear will disappear. Double your failure rate in order to accelerate your success.

" Prayer is simply a two-way conversation between you and God. "

— Billy Graham

Meeting Hard Times
with a Harder Will

"I've been driven many times to my knees by the overwhelming conviction that I had nowhere else to go. My own wisdom and all that about me seemed insufficient for that day."
- Abraham Lincoln

You were created to realize your dreams. For that reason, you will never be truly satisfied until you break down all barriers that restrict and limit your soul's aspirations.

But you have to be willing to pay the price. There **will** be a struggle. That's how you'll become stronger. You have to develop an unconquerable will.

A strong will is simply an attitude. It takes making a decision that you will not quit. It's all about the decision. Nothing much will happen in your life until you decide to burn the bridges that are holding you back.

You will go through tough times. You will have to face your fears. Everyone fears something. Though fear and trepidation may crowd your thoughts, there's always room for faith. If you are attempting to do something great and you find your knees shaking, try kneeling on them. Pray to God for strength and wisdom. Before long, you will regain the strength to fight again.

> ❝ **Decide you will not quit.** ❞

Prayer works! If you are not taking advantage of God's strength and wisdom, you aren't taking advantage of the single biggest resource in your arsenal. You can't do it by yourself. It's smart to accept his help.

Pray like it's up to God, and then work like it's up to you!

As your reliance on God grows, so will your confidence in your results. Once you start believing that you are being used by God to make great things happen, Nothing will stop you!

Put It Into Action:

Use prayer power to gain the strength and wisdom you'll need to win big.

Taking Responsibility to Take Charge of Your Life

Imagine being the captain of a sailboat at the start of an Olympic sailing final. You have been preparing thoroughly and are focused on how to take advantage of the outside conditions, the wind, the currents, and how the opposing sailboats are positioned to win the race. You can't control outside conditions. You can only control two things: what you think and what you do. How you use those two things to respond to outside conditions will determine your results in the race. You have decided to take responsibility for your results; and, consequently, you feel in control, confident, strong, and ready to win. You feel the exhilaration of the upcoming challenge. You feel great!

One of your opponents, a rookie, is not focused on what he can do to win the race. His focus is on how the wind is not blowing just right, how the currents are all wrong, and how everyone else seems to have a better sailboat and better crews than he does. The rookie is whining, complaining, and acting like a victim. He's focused on what he can't control, on the circumstances. He's not taking any responsibility. The rookie feels scared and out of control. He feels awful.

It's pretty easy to figure out who will win the race. Winning in life, like winning in a regatta, is not about what happens to you, winning is about how you handle it. It's about growing up, taking responsibility, and getting the job done.

Everything you experience today is a result of the choices you have made in the past. Whatever happens to you for the rest of your life is up to you. You are in control. You are the Captain of your own ship. You can make your life-ship drift aimlessly, or you can take your life-ship wherever you please.

"Stop making excuses and start moving to the top."

The moment you accept total responsibility for your life is the moment you grow up. Most people blame all of their problems on other people and on circumstances. They say life is not fair. People who act that way have simply never grown up. Mentally, they are still waiting for Mommy or Daddy to bail them out of their self-imposed challenges.

The next time that you are in a tough situation, rather than blaming your circumstances, say, "I am responsible, and I will fix this situation." As soon as you declare yourself responsible, your whole mental state shifts from victim mentality to victor mentality. The words "I am responsible" instantly make negative feelings and emotions vanish. Whenever you feel down, say "I am responsible," and watch what happens to your emotions. You'll be amazed!

You can't effectively set and achieve goals if you are in a negative state of mind. But once you take responsibility, you free yourself up mentally and emotionally, and you can start channeling all of your energy to the job at hand. The key is to accept responsibility.

From now on, when circumstances are not ideal, either accept that you are not willing to do what it takes to create a better life and quit complaining, or accept the risk and the price of creating a better life. Replace complaining with taking massive action. You'll feel a lot better. Guaranteed!

Start seeing yourself as the master of your own fate. Focus on the future and on what you can do right now to achieve it. The more responsibility you accept, the more control you'll feel and the happier you'll be. Take responsibility and watch your life change.

Put It Into Action:

Decide to stop blaming others for your circumstances and decide to start accepting responsibility for your life.

" Victory belongs to the most persevering. "

— Napoleon Bonaparte

You are Closer to Success than You Think

You are designed with all the resources needed to make your fondest dreams come true. You only need to learn how to condition your mind for success. Ninety percent of the input we get in the world is negative, and ninety percent of the things we tell ourselves are negative. So, it is critical to learn techniques to replace the negative with positive.

In life, you don't get what you want. You get what you are. The best way to improve yourself is to change what goes into your mind. You are a product of what goes into your mind. What you think determines what you do. What you do determines what you accomplish.

Olympic Athletes understand this. We know that what goes into our mind will ultimately determine how well we do in our competition. Think of each thought as a computer "bit," the smallest unit of information possible. Many thoughts add up to become beliefs. What we believe determines how high we will go. The good news is there are ways to raise your belief level.

Beliefs are extremely important. For example, in April 1954, the belief in the world was that it was impossible to run the mile in less than four minutes. Then along came Roger Bannister. Bannister did what nobody in the history of the world had ever done. He broke the four-minute mile barrier!

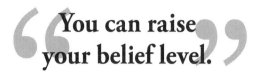

You can raise your belief level.

The phenomenal thing is that later the same month, several other athletes did it, too! Since then, over 20,000 people have run the mile in under four minutes. The only thing that changed was the belief. All of a sudden athletes knew "If Roger can do it, so can I".

Most people never attempt to do something they don't believe they can do. The good news is that you can raise your belief level through the books you read and through the people you associate with. When you hang around people who think big, you start to think big. And when people you have respect for believe in you, you start to believe in yourself.

Setting goals, visualizing the desired outcome, and finding a mentor are basic, yet critical, steps to succeeding in life. Every Olympic athlete I've ever met does all three consistently. It's just a decision. By consistently and persistently following these steps, you will reach your goals and dreams faster than 95% of the people in the world.

Put It Into Action:

Associate with winners. Read good books. Start your own personal development resource library. Find a mentor or coach.

How to Become Self Motivated

The reason most people quit on their dreams is because they have forgotten why they wanted their dream in the first place. Once you stop focusing on the "why," you start focusing on your obstacles, then become discouraged, and finally quit. The key to becoming self motivated is to find your why and to constantly focus on it. If you do that, discouragement can't get a foothold in your life and you will not quit.

Many people set goals without having a clear, compelling reason for them. You need to have strong "why's" to back up your goals. A powerful "why" is what separates a goal setter from a goal achiever. The "why" becomes the driving force that gets you into action. The "why" is the motivation. But, it is up to you to become the starter, the spark plug, if you will, for your "why." Once you get the "why" going, the "why" will get **you** going.

The best way to effectively use your "why" to become unstoppable is to create a "why" card. The "why" card is written specifically for you. You need to read your "why" card every morning and evening with power, passion, and conviction over and over for three minutes. That's how you "jump start" your why. If you do this every day, your why will automatically drive you to take massive action in the pursuit of your dream.

Fear of failure is what keeps most people from realizing their dreams. Reading your why card will give you the courage to take action in spite of your fear because if your why is big enough, the facts don't count. Initially, your why will fit on a 3x5 card. As you become crystal-clear about the life you want to create, your why might end up being several pages long. My why started out as a short card and eventually became a 30-minute cassette tape. I would listen to my why tape on the way to the gym, and it fired me up to be my best.

Focus on your 'Why.'

Here is an example of what somebody might write on their why card:

I'm willing to do whatever it takes to realize my dream because my dream will transform my life. I am financially free. By business is booming, and because of it, I am spending more and more time with my family. We live in a dream home in Colorado. We also have a winter home in southern Spain. We travel the world as a family. I see our children using the principles of success to positively impact other people's lives as they achieve their own dreams. We are donating 50% of our income to the charities of our choice. I am building a library for our local school. I'm in terrific shape. I'm making a big impact in other people's lives. I'm enjoying the fruit of my work.

Tips for Writing Your Why Card:

- Your "why" card needs to be written in the present tense, it needs to be filled with action verbs, and it needs to make you feel empowered and strong. If it doesn't, you are not dreaming big enough. Your dream needs to take your breath away. If the thought of your dream doesn't make you get up at a different time, make you read the books, listen to the tapes, and hang around different people, it's not big enough.

- Your "why" will empower you to act differently. It will make you carry yourself differently. It will change you. It will make you better. That's why your dream needs to be bigger than you currently are. It has to make you grow. The dream gives your life a purpose.
- Stop focusing on your past. Start focusing on your "why." Remember, you have enormous God-given power to make your dream a reality. You just have to believe that you were created to make your dream a reality. I challenge you to find your why, to read it daily, to share it with the world, and to make your life an adventure.

Put It Into Action:

Write and use your "why" card, so you can build and create a better life. Use your "why" card to make you relentless in the pursuit of your dreams.

" He who refuses to embrace an
opportunity loses the prize as
surely as if he had failed. "

— William James

Probabilities and Possibilities

Whether I'm speaking to 25 people in a boardroom or 10,000 people in an arena, I finish my speeches by saying, "What are the chances that someone like me was going to make it to the Olympics? I wasn't a great athlete; I didn't get started until I was 21 years old. To top it off, I live in hot and humid Houston, and I chose to compete in the luge, for Pete's sake! What are the chances? One in a million? One in ten million? I probably had a better chance to win the lottery!"

"I was just an ordinary kid with an extraordinary dream. I wasn't a big shot. I was just a little shot that kept on shooting. And that's something you can do, too. If you make a decision to become a little shot who keeps on shooting, the world is yours."

Believe it or not, the secret to creating an extraordinary life is right in those words. Most people look at their dreams and start calculating the odds of them ever happening. They can tell you the probabilities and that number is what keeps them from even getting started. They don't understand that the probability at any one time has nothing to do with success, because if you don't even get started, the probability of success is zero. They don't realize that they can change the probabilities.

Every time you take action in the pursuit of your dream, you're increasing the probabilities of reaching it. It's all up to you. **You have control over the probabilities.** Once you buy into that, it's easier to make a decision to take massive action. Understanding that makes it easier to commit to your dream. Once you commit to your dream and make a decision to do whatever it takes for as long as it takes, the probability of success increases dramatically. Why? Because 99% of the people will **never** do whatever it takes!

When I called the people in Lake Placid to ask for help in getting started in the luge, the guy on the phone laughed at me. He said I was way too old to get started. He said, "If you want to do it at your age and in only four years, it will be brutal. Nine out of ten people quit!" When I heard that, I got excited. I got excited because I could see the opportunity. And I simply decided that quitting would not be an option for me.

Once I made that decision, all I had to do was to outlast everyone else! The guy on the phone saw my probability as one out of ten. But I saw it as 100% (as long as I was willing to outlast everyone else). Four years and a few broken bones later, I was competing in the Olympics (it wasn't quite that simple, but focusing on the possibility got me to do what I needed to do to become an Olympian).

Stop focusing on the probabilities. Focus on the possibility. Ask yourself, "What is my dream? Is it a dream that takes my breath away? Is it something that excites me and gives meaning to my life?" And if it is, ask yourself, "If it is possible, then why not me?"

Don't focus on the probabilities. Focusing on the probabilities will kill your confidence. Once you lose your confidence, it's easy to quit. And stop hanging around people who talk about being realistic. Realistic people live boring lives and **never** do **anything** exciting. Start hanging around winners. Hang around achievers. I have **never** heard a real winner talk about being realistic. Think about three people you truly admire. I guarantee you that they did not get where they are by being realistic!

Focus on your dream, listen to your gut feeling, and follow your heart wholeheartedly. Ask yourself, "Why not me? Why not now?" and, "What can I do right now to get me closer to my dream?" When you ask yourself the right questions, focus on the possibilities, and hang around like-minded people, your confidence will soar and you'll be on the road to realizing your dream. Do that, and at the end of your life, you will be able to look back and say, "I lived a magnificent life!"

" **The ladder of success is best climbed by stepping on the rungs of opportunity.**

— Ayn Rand

"You always win by taking the journey. The journey transforms you. The person you become is the true purpose of the journey.

— Ruben Gonzalez

PART VII
BECOMING ALL THAT YOU CAN BE AS YOU CROSS THE FINISH LINE

Four years of training for four luge runs that take less than a minute each. But you're an Olympian forever. Pursue your dream, and when you realize your dream, no one will ever be able to take it from you.

> **"Failure is simply the opportunity to begin again, this time more intelligently."**

— Henry Ford

A Technique
Every Champion Uses

There is something that every professional athlete, Olympic athlete, professional golfer, astronaut, and every top achiever does to win more often. They use a technique called *visualization.*

Visualization is just a fancy word for 'vividly imagining' what it will feel like when you reach your goal. What will it look like? What will it sound like? What will it smell like? What will it taste like? What will it feel like? Visualization is your mind's sneak preview of coming attractions. It's a mental blueprint of your future.

Even before competing in my first Olympics, I might have been jogging, lifting weights, eating dinner, or simply walking in the mall, but you know what was going on in my head?

In my mind, I was walking into the Opening Ceremonies, and the crowd was cheering wildly. To the right, I could see the Olympic Flag waving. Behind me, I could see the Olympic Torch. I could hear the orchestra playing the Olympic Anthem – my favorite song in the whole wide world! I was there! High-fiving my teammates and shouting, "We made it guys! We made it! It was worth it! We're

Olympians!" I could feel the cold wind blowing on my face, the snow hitting my face, the tears of joy running down my cheeks, and the goose bumps running up my neck, my cheeks, and my forehead. I was there!

> **"There are miracles with your name on them."**

Four years later, when I was actually walking into the Opening Ceremonies, it was just like when I'd imagined it. Only a **hundred** times better!

The mind can't tell the difference between something you are vividly imagining with all your senses and something that is actually happening. By regularly picturing what you intend to do, you become like a guided missile that can't miss its target. You rekindle the flame of belief and literally become unstoppable.

Visualization helps you develop the intense belief in yourself you'll need to take consistent and persistent action on your goals and aspirations. There are miracles with your name on them. Miracles you were designed to go out and make happen, miracles that are just waiting for you to heed the call—waiting for you to dare to take the journey to achieve them.

By constantly seeing your miracle in your mind's eye, you will strengthen the belief and the desire you need to make the journey. Do this and success will be a matter of time.

Put It Into Action:

Regularly spend time vividly imagining what it will feel like when you actually realize your goals and dreams. Get all your senses involved and allow yourself to get emotional.

How to Benefit From Other People's Success

Have you ever had a mentor or someone more experienced than you tell you something that made no sense? Did you listen to them, or did you try to re-invent the wheel?

My first time in Lake Placid was in the spring of 1984, right after watching the Sarajevo Winter Olympics on TV. We trained for a few weeks on wheels (the wheel training was done to learn the fundamentals of steering a luge). Later that year, in the winter of 1984, I returned to Lake Placid for my first ice training. Luging on ice is completely different from luging on wheels. On ice, there is hardly any traction; therefore, ice luge is much more unforgiving. It's like the difference between walking and ice skating.

When you are first learning how to luge on ice, the coaches have you slide from the bottom third of the track, where you're only traveling at about 30 miles per hour. As your skill improves, they slowly move you up the track. It takes about 100 runs before the coaches will let you slide from the top of the track.

My goal for my first luge season back in the winter of 1984 was to be able to luge from the Men's Start at the top of the track by the end of the season. My goal for my second season was to qualify to race in the Lake Placid World Cup. My plan for the second season was to spend all winter in Placid, take as many runs as possible, and see if I could qualify for the race that was to be held on February, 1986.

As soon as I got to Lake Placid, my coaches set me straight. They said, "If you stay here all winter, your progress will be very slow. If you want to progress fast, you need to be constantly challenged.

> **"Don't let pride get in the way of your dream."**

If you train at any track for more than two weeks, you'll get bored. Once you get bored, you stop improving. You need to train here for two weeks, then two weeks in each of several tracks in Europe, **then** come back to Lake Placid, and you'll be a whole second faster."

What they were telling me made absolutely no sense to me. How could training in Europe possibly help my times in Lake Placid? But I'd promised myself that I would humble myself to my coaches' leadership and not question them. I had promised myself that I would take **all** of their advice on faith. After all, who was I to question the U.S. Olympic Coaches? That season, I trained in Europe. I learned different things from every track. And when I returned to Placid, I was a full second faster than before. The athletes who didn't listen to the coaches and decided to train in Lake Placid all season never caught up to me.

Thank God I was smart enough to listen to my coaches. If I had let my pride get in the way, I might have missed out on competing in the 1988 Calgary Olympics. Don't let pride get in the way of achieving your goals and dreams. Find a mentor who has done what you aspire to do and then faithfully follow their advice. You'll be glad you did.

How to Succeed When Conditions Change

What do you say to yourself when market conditions or your work or home conditions change? Do you see change as a good thing or as a bad thing?

One of my old success CDs says, "Success is about change – not challenge." I was never sure what that meant until one day, when I was playing racquetball with my good friend, Todd Guest.

Todd is Chief Accounting Officer of an energy company based here in Houston. Todd was killing me on the racquetball court. Todd has this powerful slam serve that I just could not return. He was scoring all these easy points, and he beat me the first three games straight.

I started to feel frustrated, then sorry for myself, and finally, mad. My anger caused me to completely change my game. I unconsciously transformed my style from a finesse game to a speed and power game. I won the fourth game handily and Todd said, "Looks like you made an adjustment and it worked."

We took a short break to get some water and started talking

about success, change, and how it is so important to make an adjustment when you are not getting the desired results. Todd used his son as an example.

Todd's oldest son, Kyle, is a very good baseball player. Kyle's been playing on All Star baseball teams for as long as I can remember. We were talking about Kyle's success in baseball, and Todd pointed out how successful baseball hitters constantly adjust to different pitchers and different circumstances. The same is true in any sport. Watch any tennis match and notice how one player wins the first set, then the other player adjusts and takes the second, and so on.

The same is true in luge. You need to be ready to adjust to changing weather conditions and to changes in track conditions. The quicker you adjust, the better off you are.

" **You can get bitter or you can get better.** "

Conditions change constantly—at work, in the marketplace, at home, and in life. When conditions change, you have two choices. You can get bitter or you can suck it up, make an adjustment, and get better. Success is about change, not challenge. Those who adjust first usually overcome the obstacle and are more likely to win.

Do you accept change? If you do, you need to stop. Accepting change is putting up with change. If you are only accepting change, you still have a bad attitude, and you'll never be your best if your attitude is negative.

You need to start embracing change. You need to welcome change, because changing conditions make you better at whatever you do. Changing conditions give you an opportunity to shine because, whenever there is change, whoever adapts first, wins. Change keeps the game interesting. Start praying for change. It gives you a chance to shine.

I'd like to tell you that I went on to win the fifth racquetball game, but Todd adjusted to my power game and won the last game. Todd, I'll get you next time!

Put It Into Action:

Embrace change. Welcome change. Look at change as an opportunity to surpass your competition.

" Small opportunities are often the beginning of great enterprises. "

— Demosthenes

Take Advantage of Opportunities

Opportunity is everywhere. You just have to keep your eyes open and focus on finding it. Once you spot an opportunity, if you decide you are willing to do whatever it takes, it's only a matter of time before you get what you want.

In November 1987, we had just arrived at the luge track in St. Moritz, Switzerland. We were about to begin training and qualifying for the World Cup Race that weekend. The International Luge World Cup Circuit is like a traveling circus. Every week, you see the same group of athletes at a different track. We typically travel on Mondays, train and qualify Tuesday through Friday, race on the weekends, and then travel to the next track.

As soon as we got to the St. Moritz track, I noticed something was different. There were only three sleds signed up in the doubles competition. Doubles luge is a wild sport consisting of two athletes lying on the same sled. They both steer, but only the top man can see. The top man gives body signals to the bottom man to tell him when to steer. It takes years to develop the trust, communication skills, and teamwork required to do well in doubles. I'd never done it. I'm a singles luge racer. But only three sleds! What an opportunity!

I ran to my best luge buddy, Pablo Garcia of Spain, and excitedly told him, "This is our chance! We'll never have another opportunity like this! We **have** to find a doubles sled and race. If one of those other three sleds crashes, we'll have a World Cup Medal!"

Pablo's no dummy. He saw the opportunity right away. But we still had to talk Coach into letting us race. We told him the opportunity was too good to pass up. It was even worth the risk of injury. Coach said, "If you can find a doubles sled in **this** town, you've got my blessing.

Finding a doubles sled in St. Moritz was going to be a real challenge. Even though they have a track, St. Moritz is not a big luge town. They love bobsled and skeleton (head-first luge), but hardly anyone in St. Moritz does the luge. That didn't matter to us. We were determined to do whatever it took to make it happen.

> **"Trust your intuition and take decisive action."**

I spent two days knocking on doors all around the town asking the locals if they had a doubles sled we could borrow. I was cold-calling in a foreign country – in a town that does not like lugers! They speak German in St. Moritz. I don't. But it didn't matter. When you want something bad enough, the facts don't count. You just do it. I knocked on the doors, regurgitated a German phrase I had memorized – *"Haben sie ein doppelsitzer rennrodeln schlitten fur die weltcup renn?"* (Do you have a doubles sled for the World Cup Race?) and hoped they nodded!

Eventually, I found a man who had a 20 year-old rusted out sled in his shed. He agreed to let us borrow it. We spent the next two days getting that antique sled race-ready.

On race day, everyone came out to see Pablo and I kill ourselves trying to do doubles. We almost did! We were on the verge of crashing the whole way down. But we finished the race, placed fourth, and actually received a World Cup Medal (we'd never even seen a 4th place medal before; they usually only award medals to the top three finishers), got out pictures in the paper, and best of all, we earned so many World Cup Points for coming in fourth, that by season's end, we had a world ranking of 14th in the doubles!!!

The following week, the word that Pablo and I had taken fourth in the World Cup spread like wildfire in the luge circuit. Some of the athletes who had not shown up in St. Moritz heard about what we had done, but passed off our victory saying, "we were lucky." Pablo and I explained to them that "luck had nothing to do with it." We simply had seen an opportunity and made a decision to do whatever it took to win, and in the end, won! We made our own luck.

I guarantee that if you develop that attitude – the attitude that you will go for it and give it your all, your life will be a lot more fun. People will be amazed at the things you accomplish. Jump and the net will appear. It really will!

Put It Into Action:

Take advantage of opportunities. Don't second guess yourself. If you feel an opportunity is right for you, take immediate action. You'll be glad you did!.

"I always tried to turn every disaster into an opportunity."

— John D. Rockefeller

How to Run Your Brain for Maximum Achievement

Remember what happened the last time you bought a car? Didn't it seem like everyone was suddenly driving the same make, model, and even color car you had just bought? You know why that happened? Because buying a car was an emotional experience that caused your brain to start focusing on that model and color of car. We are wired that way… that's just how the brain works.

The latest findings scientifically prove that by regularly writing your goals down, visualizing your intended result, and passionately saying affirmations, you actually physically change your brain's neurons and hard-wire your subconscious mind to focus like a guided missile on reaching your dreams and goals.

At the base of the brain, where it connects with the spinal cord, is a region called the Reticular Activation System (RAS). The RAS acts like a filter that decides which thoughts to focus on at any one time. We need this filter system because every second, there are about 8 million bits of information flowing through our brain. There has to be a way to filter out the noise! You can think of the RAS as the brain's gatekeeper to conscious thought. It's critical to your future that you learn how to get messages past the gatekeeper.

So, what causes some of the messages to get through the RAS

and others to get blocked out? Whatever is important to you at the time and whatever you are currently focusing on gets through. If your focus is to buy a house in the Rockies, your RAS will automatically filter in thoughts that will help you get that house – people who might help you, opportunities to make it happen, or resources that you might need. What that means is that the more you keep your goals "top of mind," the more your subconscious mind will work to reach them.

That's why writing your goals down every day, visualizing your intended outcome, and regularly saying affirmations is so important! Because doing those things help you focus your subconscious mind on what's important to **you**.

Visualization taps into the creative powers of the subconscious mind. If you want massive success, you need to learn how to get your subconscious mind to work for you. Visualization focuses your subconscious mind to look for those resources. It draws you to the people, resources, and opportunities that will help you reach your goals.

Once you learn how to get your subconscious mind working for you, your life will start changing dramatically. You'll find yourself waking up in the morning filled with great ideas that will help you reach your goals. You'll start meeting people who can help you realize your dreams. You'll be like a magnet that attracts favorable conditions. People will start saying you are lucky!

So, get started right now. Schedule time daily to write your goals, to vividly imagine what success will be like for you, and to get in front of a mirror and passionately tell yourself that you "**Will make your dreams come true!**" And you will!

Put It Into Action:

Schedule time daily to write your goals and to vividly imagine what success will feel like.

The Olympic Attitude...
Whatever it Takes!

Why do some people pursue their dreams while others bury their dreams? It comes down to belief and desire. It depends on whether you believe it's possible, whether you believe you can do it, and whether you want the dream enough to do whatever it takes.

Let's say you believe it's possible and you think there's a good chance you can pull it off ...now, what steps do you need to take to make it happen?

Step number one is the willingness to take the risk. Many people are able, but few are willing. You see, you always have to give something up in order to get something better. Most people are not willing to give anything up. They are not willing to make any sacrifices. They expect success to just fall on their lap.

That's just not how life works. There's no free lunch. Not only do you have to be willing to go for it, but you have to be willing to do whatever it takes. Let's break that last sentence down...

You have to be **willing**. Willing means that you are open minded. Open minded means you are not judgmental. It means not making any excuses. It means you are open to doing whatever might be required.

Whatever it takes is a level of commitment. Being committed means you have made a decision that you will continue to pursue your goal no matter what the consequences.

When you have a clear objective and are committed, you'll naturally start doing the things that will move you toward your objective, and you'll naturally stop doing the things that move you away from your objective.

When you have a dream you are willing to fight for, the process takes care of itself. Whatever it takes is not just a level of commitment. It's a HIGH level of commitment. And, believe it or not, it's the *lowest* level of commitment that will guarantee that you will realize your dream.

Let me explain. In reaching your dream, whether it be to become financially free, or to buy a new car, or to be able to take your family to Disneyland for two weeks, or to get your PhD...no matter what your dream is, you have to be willing to do whatever it takes.

Here's why. If realizing your dream involves 64 items, 64 things you possibly have to do, you have to be willing to do all 64 of them. If you're only willing to do 63 of them, but not #64, then #64 will be your undoing and you can kiss your dream goodbye. It's an attitude thing.

Life will seldom ask you to do all 64 things. But you don't know which ones you'll have to do, so you'd better be willing to do all 64. The "whatever it takes" attitude will help you do the required items so well that success will be assured.

The trick is to be willing to do whatever it takes with no guarantees of success. Only then is success possible.

Put It Into Action:

Make a decision that you are willing to do whatever it takes to realize your goals and dreams.

Your Choices Will Impact Many Generations

Whom you associate with will determine what habits you acquire, and your habits determine your results. Believe it or not, whom you associate with could have an impact on many generations.

A few weeks ago at church, our preacher was talking about how the choices we make could influence our descendants' lives. He kept going back to an example of two men (Max Jukes and Jonathan Edwards) who lived in New England in the 18th century and how the choices they had made (including whom they associated with) made a huge impact for four generations and thousands of descendents.

Max Jukes had a drinking problem that kept him from holding a steady job. It also kept him from showing much concern for his wife and children. He would disappear sometimes for days and return drunk. Max Jukes chose a life of unprincipled behavior and crime.

Among his 1,200 descendants were: 440 lives of outright debauchery, 310 paupers and vagrants, 190 public prostitutes, 130 convicted criminals, 100 alcoholics, 60 thieves and 7 murderers. A pretty depressing family tree, to say the least!

Jonathan Edwards is regarded as one of the most brilliant and influential men of American history. He was a gifted pastor and exceptional theologian. Edwards' preaching ignited the flame that led to the Great Awakening, and he later served as the president of Princeton College.

"Associate with winners." Among his male descendants were: 300 clergymen, missionaries, or theology professors, 120 college professors, 60 doctors, 60 authors, 30 judges, 14 college presidents, 3 U.S. congressmen, 1 vice-president of the United States… and one incredible Winter Olympian—a special guy who helped me compete in the 2002 Olympics (You'll read about him in the next chapter).

Ninety percent of your success will come from whom you associate with. Are you associating with the type of people who will lead you to make positive choices and create an awesome life and an awesome legacy, or are you associating with the type of people who will lead you to a life of mediocrity? It's your choice!

Put It Into Action:

Associate with people you respect. Learn and apply their success habits.

How to Make a Difference in Other People's Lives

One definition of character is how you act when no one is looking at you. Another definition of character is: how you treat people who could not possibly help you in any way.

How you treat people who cannot help you says a lot about you. Do you ignore them? Do you walk over them? Or do you encourage them and help them out?

What difference does it make? It makes a huge difference. Character is a big part of leadership because people are more likely to follow and trust you if you are a person of character. They will want to develop long-term relationships with you. If you're in sales (and by the way, **everyone** is in sales), they will buy more often and buy more product from you. Your whole quality of life improves if you are a person of character.

One of the worst luge crashes of my career came at a terrible time – three days before the luge race at the Salt Lake City Olympics. I didn't even see my crash coming. It caught me completely off guard. For the first time in my life, I was completely disoriented. I remember seeing the sky twice and hitting the bottom of the track twice. The whole time, I was thinking, "Please, God, don't let me break any bones! I'm racing in the Olympics in three days!"

Thank goodness, I didn't break anything. Unfortunately, my sled was a mess. The steel runners were gouged and scratched so badly that I didn't think I would be able to fix them in time for the race. The medics picked me up and drove me back to the Men's Start House at the top of the mountain.

I walked into the start house holding my sled. My face must have been ashen because all the other athletes there looked at me and starting mumbling in different languages. Then, something incredible happened. Jonathan Edwards walked right up to me, took a look at my sled, and said, "Give me 30 minutes and a file and I'll have your steels looking like new." Jonathan is actually a descendant of Jonathan Edwards from the previous chapter!

I didn't even know Jonathan Edwards! Jonathan had competed in the luge in the 1994 Lillehammer Winter Olympics. In Salt Lake City, Jonathan was coaching the Bermuda Luge Team.

Jonathan had nothing to gain from helping me. He helped me because he has a big heart; he's a person of character; a person who is genuinely interested in helping other people out. He's just a terrific guy. Jonathan got me out of a terrible situation. He just showed up out of nowhere, kind of like a guardian Angel.

It's very unusual to find someone like that. You want to be around people like that. What if we all strived to be a little bit more like Jonathan? Would we have more influence over everyone we meet? Would the world be a better place?

Character counts. Big time!

Put It Into Action:

Strive to become a person of character. Help others succeed. Touch other people's lives. Become the type of person you'd want your kids to be around.

Success is Like Learning How to Ride a Bike

As I was teaching my six-year-old daughter, Gabriela, how to ride a bike, I realized that she was going through all the challenges and emotions I went through when learning how to luge.

She was going through all the emotions anyone goes through when they are learning something new… hope, fear, trepidation, self-doubt, and finally exhilaration and pride that comes from pushing yourself and accomplishing something you never did before.

On the first day, Gabriela was excited and filled with anticipation as we drove to our training ground—the church parking lot. Her excitement quickly turned to fear and doubt after falling two or three times from her bike. Gabriela's a pretty tough cookie, but after a few falls, she started stalling. She didn't want to get back on that "mean" bike.

When she was ready to call it quits, I realized how important it is to have a coach. As her coach, I was able to encourage her and push her through the fear stage. I constantly corrected and encouraged Gabriela as I taught her how to balance herself on the bike.

Gabriela and Gracen. Persistence always pays off.

This took a while and felt like tough love because she was afraid throughout the whole process.

Whenever you are doing something challenging and new, it's critical to have a coach or a mentor to get you through the tough phase. You especially need help in the beginning to keep yourself from quitting. I never would have made it to the Olympics without my coach. He kept me in the game long enough for me to learn the skills and gain self confidence.

Gabriela didn't make much progress on day two. Her position was a bit better, she was a little bit looser, but she was still falling after only 10 feet. The main reason she was falling was that as soon as she started to lose balance, her fear would cause her to freeze and she would stop pedaling. At that point, I thought it would take another week before Gabriela would get it.

On the third day, I focused on getting Gabriela to continue pedaling no matter what. About 5 minutes into the lesson. I let

Gabriela's bike go and she just kept on pedaling. Gabriela rode out about 30 feet, made a big loop back, and started coming back toward me. She must not have realized that she was riding on her own, because when she saw me, her eyes got as big as saucers, she quit pedaling, and down she went. But, you should have seen her after that! From that moment, on she was on cloud nine and all she could say was, "I can't believe I did it! I did it! I can't believe it! Thank you, Daddy!"

Now, Gabriela had had a taste of success. She could see light at the end of the tunnel. With a little help from her coach, she had worked through the fear stage, and now all we had to do was a little fine tuning. Gabriela is brand new at this. She is not confident on the bike yet. Her confidence will come from practicing her bike riding skills. Confidence is not a result of faking it until you make it. Confidence comes from proper practice and mastery of your skills.

Doing something new is always hard in the beginning. Growing and developing yourself so you can succeed is tough. That's why it's critical to have someone to encourage and help you in the beginning. Once you get through the fear stage, the fun begins and you will experience pride and joy at having accomplished something you'd never done before. If you practice your new skill and you master your new skill, you will become confident.

This stuff applies to anything - riding a bike, luging, skiing, learning how to speak another language, using new sales and prospecting techniques, playing the piano, etc.

Put It Into Action:

Is fear of failure holding you back from being your best? If it is, attack your fear by getting someone else to help you work through the fear. Don't try to do it all on your own. Once you learn the new skill, practice it, master it, and enjoy the fruits of being confident in your new skill.

" My persistence is the measure of the belief I have in myself. "

— Walt Disney

One Step at a Time

I just got back from a climbing trip on Mt. Rainier. When you first see the mountain, you wonder how anyone could climb so high. You are excited and apprehensive at the same time. After all, it's a completely new experience. You're totally outside your comfort zone—especially if you're a flatlander from Houston.

Fortunately, we had experienced guides to help us along the way (one of them had just climbed Mt. Everest). Our attitude was to listen to the guides and do everything they said—the proper mentor-mentee relationship.

The guides taught us two techniques we would need right away—pressure breathing and the rest step. It is much harder for oxygen to be absorbed into your lungs at high altitudes because of the low air pressure. So, we were taught to inhale deeply and to purse our lips as we exhaled to increase the air pressure in our lungs and "push" the oxygen into the lungs. It takes conscious effort to do this, but as they said, it's like putting money in the bank because by pressure breathing, we are keeping our cells and muscles

---

Climbing Mt. Rainier one step at a time...

well oxygenated.

Conserving energy as you are climbing the mountain is very important. The rest-step is a special technique that saves a lot of our energy. As you step up the mountain, you lock your lower leg straight for a second so all your body weight is being supported by your bones, not your leg muscles. When you're carrying a 40 pound backpack, energy conservation becomes a big deal.

These techniques slow you down considerably, but they allow you to be able to climb for long periods of time without stopping. It turns out that climbing a mountain is a lot like running a marathon—it's all about energy management and pacing.

It took me about three hours to figure out my ideal pace. You want to move steadily but not so fast to where you lose your breath and have to stop. Once I figured out my ideal pace, my whole focus was on taking the next step. One hundred percent of my focus was on planting my foot on the next footprint as we climbed up a snowfield that looked like a black diamond ski run. One...step... at...a...time. Breathing hard all the way, but just short of being out of breath...one...step...at...a...time.

We did not even look up at the scenery. We couldn't. Doing so would have thrown us off balance and could have made us fall. We just focused on the next step. Pressure breathe, rest step, pressure breathe, rest step, over and over again. After each hour of climbing, our guide would make us stop for a 15-minute break. We would drop our backpacks, turn around, and be amazed at how much altitude we had gained... one...step...at...a...time. We were climbing at about 1,000' an hour. One...step...at...a...time.

Our guides broke climbing Mt. Rainier (a huge mountain) into manageable goals (several one-hour climbs) and then broke those goals down into small tasks (pressure breathing and rest-stepping). As long as we focused 100% on the tasks, the goals and the dream took care of themselves.

Whenever we lost focus or made a mistake, our guides were right there to help us out. We never would have been able to climb the mountain without our guides. Our mountain guides had the experience and the expertise to get us where we could not go on our own.

No matter how huge your dreams seem, if you break them down into manageable goals, then break the goals into simple tasks, relentlessly focus on the tasks, and rely on an experienced coach or mentor, you'll be amazed at how much you accomplish.

Put It Into Action:

Break your goals down into small manageable tasks. Focus on accomplishing your tasks one step at a time, and find a mentor or coach who can take you to heights you could never reach on your own.

> **Take the first step in faith. You don't have to see the whole staircase, just take the first step.**

— Martin Luther King Jr.

Dream – Struggle – Victory

Back when I was in grade school, my dad encouraged me to study the lives of successful people. He said, "Success leaves clues. Read biographies and you'll figure out what works in life."

I've been a student of success ever since. I've read countless biographies, and I've found them all to be very similar. They are all the story of someone who had a dream, faced a struggle, and finally had a victory. Dream, struggle, victory. Dream, struggle, victory and then someone decided to a book about them.

We all have dreams. What made those people different is they had the guts to take action. The dream was a call to action – an inner longing to strike out on an adventure. They chose to heed the call and take the journey.

Choosing to take the journey takes courage. And staying the course to victory takes courage and perseverance. That's why we admire people who go for it. We admire them because they have the heart of a champion and the adventurous spirit of winners.

Something life-changing happens when you decide to take

the journey. If you refuse to quit, you will inevitably find you have hidden resources and abilities within you. You find out what you're made of.

You always win by taking the journey. The journey transforms you. Who you become is the true purpose of the journey.

Face your fear. Take the journey. Heed the call. Bite off more than you think you can chew. Do it now! You'll never be the same.

Coach and me in Germany. Find a coach or mentor
who will help you accelerate your success.

Ruben's New Adventure

Chase your dream. Never, ever quit!

It's never too late to pursue your dream. After a six year break from the luge, Ruben has returned and is in training for the 2010 Vancouver Winter Olympics. He's back on the tracks and sliding better than he ever has before.

When Ruben competes in Vancouver at the ripe old age of 47, he will achieve the remarkable feat of becoming the only person to ever compete in four Winter Olympics in four different decades (Calgary 1988, Albertville 1992, Salt Lake City 2002, Vancouver 2010).

In Vancouver he will be competing against athletes who weren't even born when Ruben raced at the 1988 Calgary Olympics. That's historic! Remember, it's never too late to get started. Make your life an adventure. Go for the Gold and never, ever quit!

Ruben's Rules for Success

» You will never achieve anything great in life until you start believing that something inside you is bigger than the circumstances you face.

» You can become great by making a decision to pursue your dream in life and by refusing to quit.

» Every success you've ever had or will ever have is the product of your courage to act and the courage to endure.

» Success is not about how much talent you have. It's about what you do with the talent you do have.

» Successful people love the battle, the challenge, and the journey. It's about knowing that you did your best.

» You will always accomplish more when you follow a coach or mentor.

» If you do whatever it takes for however long it takes, success is only a matter of time.

The Champion's Creed

Read this every morning and you are guaranteed
to have a better and more productive day.

I am a champion.

I believe in myself.

I have the will to win.

I set high goals for myself.

I have courage. I never give up.

I surround myself with winners.

I'm cool, positive, and confident.

I'm willing to pay the price of success.

I love the struggle and the competition.

I stay relaxed and in control at all times.

I focus all my energy on the job at hand.

I vividly imagine that victory will feel like.

I am a champion, and I will win.

*For a free copy of "The Champion's Creed"
visit TheChampionsCreed.com*

About the Author

Ruben Gonzalez wasn't a gifted athlete. He didn't take up the sport of luge until he was 21. Four years later and against all odds, he was competing in the Calgary Winter Olympics. At the age of 39 he was racing against 20-year-olds in the Salt Lake City Olympics! Ruben proves that ordinary people can accomplish extraordinary things.

Ruben's appeared nationally on ABC, CBS, NBC and the FOX Business channel. He's been featured in Time Magazine, BusinessWeek, and Success Magazine, as well as publications all over the world. His articles on peak-performance are read on every continent. His column "High Achievement" appears in magazines across America. Ruben's the co-star of the movie "Pass It On," a full-length feature film about what it really takes to succeed in life.

Ruben is one of the most popular speakers in the America. His client list reads like a Who's Who of Corporate America: Coca-Cola, Dell, Shell Oil, Continental Airlines, the Million Dollar Round Table, Farmers Insurance, Ortho McNeal, Blue Cross Blue Shield, Wells Fargo, ERA Realtors, and even The U.S. Treasury Department! Ruben is hailed by speaking legends Zig Ziglar, Denis Waitley, and Tom Hopkins as a leader of a new generation of personal development speakers.

Visit TheOlympicSpeaker.com to watch his great videos, read his articles on success, and sign up for his free newsletter.

Book Ruben
for Your Next Event

Ruben travels the world entertaining, educating, and inspiring his audiences to realize their goals and dreams. He speaks about leadership, goal-setting, and overcoming challenges as you pursue your goals. Ruben uses his personal Olympic stories to illustrate all his points.

To book Ruben to speak at your next meeting, conference, or function, contact:

Olympic Motivation
832-689-8282
www.TheOlympicSpeaker.com

Special Free Bonus

Receive Ruben's monthly e-newsletter, designed to help you put what you learned from this book into practice!

Watch Ruben's 33 minute demo video filled with success lessons that will help you reach the top.

"Success is like wrestling a gorilla. You don't quit when you're tired. You quit when the gorilla is tired."

— Robert Strauss